EMERGING FROM THE TRENCHES

Truths from a mother whose world has been refined by autism.

JENNIFER HAYWORD

HUGO HOUSE PUBLISHERSHERS, LTD.

Emerging From the Trenches: *Truths from a mother whose world has been refined by autism.*

© 2019 Jennifer Hayword. All rights reserved.

No portion of this book may be reproduced mechanically, electronically, or by any other means, including photocopying, without written permission of the publisher. It is illegal to copy this book, post it to a website, or distribute it by any other means without permission from the publisher.

ISBN: 978-1-948261-21-0

Library of Congress Control Number:2019911043

Cover Design and Interior Layout: Ronda Taylor, www.heartworkpublishing.com

Cover Image Credit: Jennifer Hayword

Hugo House Publishers, Ltd.

Denver, Colorado
Austin, Texas
www.HugoHousePublishers.com

Contents

Introduction—The Shape We Are In vii

PART I—KNOCKED DOWN

1   The Lies People Tell You 1

2   Hello, My Name is Autism. 5

3   The Awakening 9

4   Swimming Pools and Padded Rooms 15

5   It's a Red Blotch / No, It's an Elephant 19

6   Acknowledgement. 25

PART II—DIGGING IN

7   Death, Taxes, and Autism. 31

8   Ryder Says, "Adapt" 37

9   Ryder Says, "Hold on Tight". 43

10   It's BROKEN! 49

11   Screw the Cake and Balloons 55

12   The Isolation is Real 59

13   We Have Our Reasons .65

14	How About Those Doctors?	71
15	To Medicate or Not to Medicate	75
16	I am Mother, and I am Guilty of Giving Into Manipulative Behavior	79
17	Literally, Dude	83
18	If They Only Had a Brain…Or Some Manners	87

PART III—GETTING BACK UP

19	The Other Jennifer	93
20	Double Ds and Triple Ps	97
21	Ha-ku-na Ma-ta-ta	101
22	Imaginative Play	107
23	Let's be Honest About Self-Esteem	111
24	My Precious	115
25	Caution, Autism Ahead	117
26	Amazingly Autistic	123
27	PB&J Posse	127
28	The Four Letter "F" Word	131

Afterword	135
Acknowledgements	137
About the Author	139
Contact the Author	141

Dedication

I dedicate this book to the generations of the future. May this book be a part in making your world more aware and accepting of each other's differences.

Introduction—
The Shape We Are In

WHEN WE PICTURE AUTISM, THE SHAPE WE USUALLY SEE IS ONE PIECE of a puzzle. Sometimes the piece is blue, sometimes rainbow colored, but a puzzle piece it is. I think that depicting autism as a puzzle piece is profoundly correct.

Most people say the puzzle piece represents the autistic child. I have no beef with that. But for our family the puzzle piece also represents what it is like to *live* with an autistic child. Life with a child on the "spectrum" one day is as smooth as the edge of an outer puzzle piece, but the next day it is bumpy with ups and downs like an inner piece. Wait, that's wrong. Let's change that. Life with an autistic child can be smooth one *minute*, directly followed the *next minute* by completely crazy, curvy ups and downs! It is never dull in an autistic household.

When we start a puzzle in our house, we dump all the pieces out on the middle of the table into a giant colorful, confusing heap before we begin constructing it. Many days I wake up feeling as if I am buried under that puzzle, loaded down with crazy yet colorful pieces, my life in a heap. (Those days require two headache pills followed by a few cups of coffee before 8 am.) Some days I awake with vigor and motivation, ready to tackle anything. But not always. Not most days. This is *absolutely* okay as far as I am concerned. As mother of this particular household, I have ranked organization and energy at a three on a scale of one to ten. They are really overrated.

Being puzzled also comes into play when you are a parent of an autistic child. I find myself puzzled over how in the world our son can smell the difference between sugar-free and regular Hershey's bars—the kid has a super sense. Or it puzzles me why he could say "dinosaur" at one year of age, yet it took him four years to say, "I want." There are days I can't recall whether or not I've taken a shower in twenty-four hours. Who knows? It's puzzling!

A few things are certain about the puzzle created by raising an autistic child. First, the autistic family's puzzle is alive! Second, your puzzle will be unlike any other autistic family's puzzle, and it will take a lifetime to put together just your portion of this puzzle. Each family member's contribution is important in the formation of the puzzle. Third and most important, you create the picture of what your puzzle is as you put the pieces in place with each passing day.

Our family has been fitting together this life puzzle for the past five years. Ours looks like a cross between the movies *Jumanji* and *National Lampoon's Christmas Vacation*. Our lives are constantly in a ruckus with suspense, surprise, horror, and laughter around every curve.

It is not at all like the structured Girl Scout meetings I used to lead when I had only one child. When I was a Girl Scout leader, I remember telling my daughter how important preparation was. Before each meeting we would pack extra snacks, have a backup plan in place, and have what we needed in our car to handle a flat tire or vehicle malfunction. Preparation for what it takes to raise an autistic child might only be found while battling the war on terror in the mountains of Afghanistan. I can plan my heart out, but my plans get shot down nearly every day.

A daily plan is different than strict routine, and there is entirely too much routine that comes with autism for my individual taste. However, autism thrives *on* routine, so we do our best. Autism does not do well with change, and change cannot always be controlled, so sometimes in the middle of cruising through a perfectly good daily routine, we have to slam on the brakes because…*life* happens. The tiniest unexpected change can throw an entire day off track.

There are not many solid answers for the autistic parent. An autism diagnosis for our child came with a pat on the back and a red folder full of phone numbers, websites, and packets of medical information explaining issues we

Introduction—The Shape We Are In

might come across while raising an autistic child. We also received a warning about seizures with a side glance which communicated, "Good luck." No one could tell us with 100 percent certainty why, when, what, or how any of this came to be or exactly what to expect in the future since all autistic children are different. As an autistic family, we have conditioned ourselves to keep pushing through each day, learning as we go, and fitting life together one puzzle piece at a time.

Finding humor among the most stressful days is key to survival.

If you are familiar with an autistic household, then I hope you get a few laughs from our story and some reassurance that you are not alone. If you are not familiar with an autistic household, don't fret as you read along—autism is not contagious.

We live in the South. Proper introductions are expected before one indulges in sharing personal information to others. Let me introduce you to who we are.

- William: Loving Dad
- Jennifer: Mom (aka The Mean Boss)
- Dawn: sixteen-year-old "chill" daughter and sister
- Kay: eight-year-old "sassy" daughter and sister
- Ryder: five-year-old "golden" autistic son and brother
- Logan: two-year-old "assertive" son and brother

The remainder of this little book is my point of view, my personal opinion, and personal high-lights on the engaging (and oftentimes unbridled) battle of raising our autistic son for the first five years of his life.

(Please note that parts of this book refer to marijuana and alcohol use in a humorous manner. However, both substances can impair an individual's judgement, therefore, potentially harming families. I don't condone anything which can harm families. In short, even if it's legal, it might not be the best idea.)

PART I

KNOCKED DOWN

1

The Lies People Tell You

I HEARD THE WORDS, "THINGS WILL GET BETTER," OR "IT WILL GET BETTER," from nearly every friend and family member who witnessed what we were struggling with for the first four years of Ryder's life. Those were the years before he could communicate enough for us to give him what he needed.

Once I even had a total stranger yell "It will be okay!" across the dairy food isle at a grocery store. Most people would tell me, "Things will get better," as if they were wishing on a star for me with a gaze upward and sweetness in their voice. Even if they were saying the phrase to me over the phone, I could hear the wishful thinking in their voice, which made it obvious to me they didn't even believe what they were saying. God knows I was smiling on the outside, and I would say, "Oh definitely," or "Yes, it will," when what I was really thinking was, "No! It's not that simple! You are lying! Liar! How could you know?! Do you know the future? You have no idea what my family is going through!"

Our friends and family would only witness bits and pieces of the craziness when they would come over for coffee, call to say hi, or pass us in public. Then they would speak their wish out loud for me because what they witnessed shocked them, and they didn't know what else to say. Most friends and family probably thanked God they didn't have to wrestle every day with what we were. Or maybe they assumed I didn't discipline my child. I was polite because I knew they meant well, and I loved them, but when they would try to reassure me with that wishful voice, I despised the moment and their words.

One of the best posts I have ever read on an autism forum was from a dad of an autistic child. The subject of the forum was autistics and puberty. People were chiming in left and right about how wild their autistic child's behavior and meltdowns had become once they hit puberty. This dad simply wrote, "Wait. You are telling me this gets WORSE!!????" I had a great laugh at his epiphany because I could feel his shock of realization. When you are crawling through a dark underground tunnel, barely making it, and then someone ahead of you turns around to tell you that the worst part is yet to come, you want so badly for it to all be a bad dream which you can wake from if only you punch yourself hard enough. (That is not a typo; I meant *punch* not pinch.)

When Ryder was three, a very special friend of mine approached me with the question, "Have you considered having Ryder tested for autism?"

Let me say that it takes a lot of balls to be the first one to suggest to a parent that you see something unusual within their child that they may not have noticed, especially when the suggestion is that their dear child may be neurologically offbeat, but my friend loved us enough to take the risk. She came to visit us after we had taken her advice and had confirmed Ryder's autism. Although she had always been able to find words to cheer me up in the past, during this visit she broke down crying and told me she just didn't know how to help me or what to say. Well, I didn't know what to tell her at first except, "Thank you." I really appreciated her honesty, but I found myself repeating words I despised simply to make her feel better: "It is going to get better. We will be okay."

I was lie-wishing straight through my teeth.

Our world was upside down. We were struggling to regroup. One day I did what any 21st Century struggling mother would do, and I blurted to Facebook:

> *"Imagine winning a trip to the Bahamas! You pack a few swimsuits, Google the best beaches and restaurants, and do everything else to prepare for a great vacation. As you board your plane for the trip you are excited! Then, because of an unknown and unexplainable change, your flight lands in Russia. You are in a country where you don't speak the language, you don't understand the customs, and you were expecting the warm beaches of the Bahamas*

so of course you are not properly packed. You are totally thrown off guard and have to figure out how to navigate your situation in order to gain your bearings back. That's how it feels when your child is diagnosed with autism. That's what we struggle with each day."

This is where I stress to you how important it is for parents and family members of autistics to reach out to one another because someone reached out to me while were in the thick of it, and her kindness helped me beyond what any wishful words could.

She was my neighbor whom I had lived next to for some time, and for whatever reason we had not crossed paths. Then one afternoon the kids and I were picking the wild blackberries that grew up and down our red dirt road, when she pulled up beside us in her SUV. She introduced herself, told me she not only had a twenty-year-old autistic son, but that she counseled families of autistics for a living. Their home next to us was their vacation home, so I had never met her son. I had no idea that for over a year she had been listening to Ryder's fits from the distance between our homes. She had heard his fits and *knew* he was autistic way before we did. She gave me her phone number, and told me I could call her anytime.

Not long after that day, Ryder and I were having a rough one. My husband was working out-of-town and I found myself calling my neighbor. I didn't even know what I was going to say. I just needed to talk to someone who might understand how I felt before I went nuts.

She was fantastic. She was honest. She told me her family's autism story, that her son had just graduated college, and he sang opera for a hobby. (Wow! Her son's story still gives me such a feeling of hope.)

We talked about siblings of autistics, and she warned me to not let autism put them second. It is easy to get so wrapped up in your special-needs child's life, your other children might feel benched, watching from the sidelines while mom and dad play coach to their autistic sibling.

She asked about my marriage, and we talked about the divorce rates among parents of autistics. She firmly told me to let trusted friends or family members help if they ask. My mother-in-law had been asking for months to watch Ryder while my husband and I went out, and I never took Mimi up on her offer before then because I didn't want to stress her out too much. I knew how taxing Ryder's autism could be, and I assumed that if I struggled with it as his own mother, surely another person would pull her hair out.

She gave me book suggestions and recommended a few learning tools for Ryder. I had just met this woman, but we talked for over an hour about many autism-related issues. She had been in my shoes so she could relate, and she didn't sugar-coat anything. I was so thankful I had met her. When I hung up the phone, I locked myself in my bedroom and cried a good, long-needed cry.

I have two dear friends who have each lost a son. Neither one of these friends have ever said to me, "Things will get better." When they see Ryder, they smile and say things like, "He is a ham." Or "He is sweet." Or they simply listen to me when I talk about Ryder and jokingly tell me they will take him if I ever want to get rid of him. Somewhere, I had read that coming to terms with having an autistic child is similar to the death of a child. How morbid can we be?

I strongly disagree with this comparison. I have seen what losing a son has looked like on the faces of my dear friends. How could I ever compare my challenges with raising Ryder to their loss? Perhaps what this person was trying to say was that you have to let your visions and dreams of who your child will become die away when they are diagnosed autistic. Then allow new visions to be born because your child is still physically with you, but who he or she will become is going to be different than you expected or envisioned. They will still be fantastic, beautiful, gifted and amazing, but they will be different.

We have come a long way from "Things will get better." Now friends and family tell me, "Ryder is doing so well." Or "I have noticed such a change in him." I hear the surprise and relief in their voices, but no wishful thinking, so I know they are telling the truth, and they have hope for our future.

Doubts and worries still tend to cloud my hope for Ryder's future, but hope is still there somewhere. So I just keep swimming, like Dory suggests in *Finding Nemo*. We try to keep swimming forward and only look back to compare how far ahead we have come.

Hello, My Name is Autism

"You don't want to put a label on your son" is what a person told me when we first started to tell close friends we thought Ryder may be autistic. A label? What is Ryder, a ketchup bottle? I know she loves us and she always wanted the best for us. I know those words came out of her mouth without her even thinking about them. I know her point of view was a natural reaction to how things were handled in her generation.

There are many issues older generations used to sweep under the rug from fear of being seen as different or from fear of being "labeled." In the past, if a family member was molested or raped, the victim might be urged to forget it happened and move on with their life. If a family member became pregnant out-of-wedlock, they were sent to visit their "aunt" for 9 months. Shoot, even divorce used to leave a family with a stigma. And the same went for children with uncommon mental health issues. Some would be locked in institutions their entire life. A few generations ago doctors might have urged us to lock up Ryder.

Ignoring any elephants in the room such as these does absolutely nothing to help the person and family affected.

What's the big deal anyhow? People choose to label themselves every day on social media. They are the ones sharing every bit of information about themselves and labeling themselves at the same time. They actually *want* to be labeled. You can create an entirely false identity online these days by adding labels. Want to be homosexual? No problem, change your status, and throw a few rainbow flags on your page. Want to be viewed as skinnier? No problem, photoshop your picture. Want to be called Dr.? No problem, add an M.D. after your last name on your profile and start posting nonsensical medical advice on public forums.

Can you imagine if we were all *honestly* labeled without being allowed to filter the truth? What if these 100 percent honest labels were easily accessible to anyone at any time and photo altering was never invented for our selfies? Oh, the things we wouldn't be able to hide from! My label would probably look like this:

Jennifer Hayword: (Goofy picture showing all my flaws)

Highlights and/or questionable issues: Resident of Texas, gun owner, problems with authority from a young age, married at 20, raising and homeschooling four children; eight total traffic tickets, two previous warrants for arrest, four total car accidents, and a possible partridge in a pear tree.

Education: Not a college graduate.

Negative traits: Compulsive, stubborn, too talkative, opinionated, possibly psychotic.

Positive traits: To be determined.

(I swear this makes me sound much worse than I was and currently am.)

As much as people like to label themselves on social media, because society is so judgmental, no one *really* wants to be labeled with the truth of who they are. I wouldn't wish to stick Ryder with a label that could potentially harm him in the future. So we took our dear friend's warning into consideration, but decided that whatever was going on with Ryder wasn't a shameful thing like airing our dirty laundry and it wasn't as meaningless as labeling a ketchup bottle. Our entire family's quality of life for generations after us was at stake. What did we have to lose by reaching out to find help? If we had to slap a "label" on Ryder in order to find some help, then so be it, and the shame would be on those who would see him as less simply because he is different.

Chapter 2—Hello, My Name is Autism

I have heard autistics labeled as retarded or violent, and I have certainly heard the controversial argument that a majority of school shooters were autistic. These labels placed upon autistics are absolutely incorrect and unfair. Society in *general* is full of retarded violent people who enjoy killing everything that moves on the realistic video games they play. Some people take things to the extreme, leaving death and destruction in their path, but not all shooters are autistic.

Still, I had an assuming person warn me not to let Ryder watch violent TV shows which portrayed mass shootings or people being slaughtered because Ryder learns and copies behavior that he sees on a regular basis. Since Ryder is a child, of course, we don't let him watch non-stop gore and violence. He would rather watch Mickey Mouse Clubhouse anyhow. What we do with *all* our children is teach them to treat both humans and guns with respect. All children should be taught a gun is used for hunting or personal protection, never to kill random people.

Ryder is *definitely not* retarded, he has only been violent to himself in the past when he is highly frustrated, and guns scare the *rip* out of him. He certainly isn't going to be the school shooter at our homeschool academy, maybe the gold medal swimmer, but not a shooter. At the same time though, a green apple tastes different than a red apple, decaf coffee is not caffeinated coffee, and autistics are different than the norms. Let's call things what they are and teach more acceptance of differences.

Labeling Ryder included a specialist placing him on either the high or low end of the spectrum. We were told Ryder has High Functioning Autism and I am stumped when it comes to understanding how the specialist came to this conclusion. Sure, he doesn't have any physical handicaps which keep him from being able to run, jump, hop, or climb, but Ryder's sensory, behavioral, social, and communicative barriers may keep him at a level where he cannot function in the world as smoothly as other children his age. On the other hand, I met an autistic child Ryder's age who doesn't have any physical handicaps, nor does he have any sensory, social, or behavioral issues. He doesn't speak at all, but he can communicate much better than Ryder can through a program on his IPad. As I communicated with the little boy and learned how expressive he was, I could see a future for this other child without as many hurdles as Ryder will have to go over, yet his mother was told her son has Low Functioning Autism.

Whatever, I am relieved we at least know what is causing Ryder's differences and struggles. Plus, I feel relieved to know my son will not be drafted into the military and put on the front lines if World War III breaks out. He simply couldn't handle the guns, noise, and commotion. Now the military might request help from Ryder due to his fantastic memory, but we will cross that bridge when we get to it.

I don't see autism as a label. I see it is as a diagnosis. Ryder's diagnosis gave us a jumping off point and a direction. Before Ryder's diagnosis we were a family without direction or a map. We didn't know where we had landed, what to look out for, or where we were going. (Ok, so we still don't know exactly where we are going, but at least now we have a direction, a map, some tools, and an idea of where we *want* to go.)

We now have information and support which helps us to be patient with each other on the rough days, all thanks to his "diagnosis."

3

The Awakening

MY HUSBAND'S JOB KEEPS HIM AWAY FROM HOME QUITE OFTEN. HIS WORK schedule is unpredictable, but through the years we have learned how to work around it. We might have Christmas in early December or Easter the weekend after the official Easter weekend. It doesn't seem to bother any of the kids, especially the years when they get Christmas presents early. However, having babies around William's work schedule has been a roller coaster ride because it's much more difficult to move around the date of a baby being born than the day we celebrate a holiday.

If you've been pregnant before, you know that by week 32 (or sooner) you are ready to be relieved of carrying such a heavy load. It's hard to do anything! It's hard to move, pee, eat, drive, and with our fourth child, Logan, it was especially hard for me to sleep. Our children have all been huge babies, the next one always been larger than its predecessor. I knew Logan was going to set the family record because at about 34 weeks into my pregnancy the circulation began to get cut off in my arms and hands from the sheer weight of him. It seemed to happen more often in the middle of the night than the daytime and the feeling of fire ants running up and down my arms and fingers could last for hours. I spent many nights in pain, quietly crying and feeling sorry for myself on the couch so I wouldn't wake up the house.

A pregnancy like that, during Ryder's early years, while trying to run a small farm with pigs, goats, chickens, dogs, cats, and horses, was a nightmare *every day*. I was *so* ready to deliver child number four. Yet I found myself asking my doctor, "Doc, is there any way we can hold off that C-section for another week so William can be here?" She thought I was joking.

My husband wasn't going to be home in time for the birth of Logan and we couldn't get around it. I knew I was in for a hospital stay of at least three full days and two nights. But no one had ever stayed with Ryder for over two hours and definitely not even close to overnight. Even though the girls were pretty good handling Ryder, we couldn't expect them to be in charge of the household and run a farm for multiple days and nights. It was too risky and probably illegal. We lived in the middle of nowhere. The closest gas station was at least fifteen minutes away by speeding car. (Which Dawn and Kay did not have a license to drive) Our closest neighbors were a few acres away if they were even home since they traveled a lot and cell phone service was dabble at its best.

My mother-in-law Mimi stepped up to the plate and agreed to stay with the kids during my extended stay at the hospital and to do her best with two-year-old Ryder, come hell or high water.

I am familiar with nesting, but preparing the house for my departure this go around was what I refer to as *My Moment of Awakening*.

I had to have the foods Ryder would eat stacked to the ceiling. Weeks before Logan's due date I sat down to make a few notes to go on the refrigerator for Mimi to access easily. I made the usual lists of daily chores or activities the girls needed to complete, and notes on where to find certain items about the house, but I also made a list of how Ryder needed things to be done in order for the days and nights to run as smooth as possible. Now we hadn't even considered Ryder might be autistic at this point. We were convinced he was a difficult child, and we put a lot of the other quirks he had, along with the speech delay, toward him being a boy.

The list I sat down to make in order to help Mimi with Ryder took on its own life, growing longer and longer. I hadn't realized how we had fallen into such a strenuous routine for every little part of the day simply because without the details being done correctly, we would have loud (and sometimes violent) fits of frustration from Ryder. (The poor baby would start scratching, biting, or tearing at his own belly or arms when he couldn't be calmed down.)

For example:
- Ryder had to have a hot bath the moment he woke up with lavender bath soap,
- followed by exactly three scrambled eggs cut up into squares and sprinkled with cheese-flavored seasoning and a glass of water to go with the eggs,
- but the water had to be served in the elephant cup, and it needed to have a packet of his probiotics put into it (without him seeing) before he sat down to eat.
- There were two particular Minnie Mouse hair bows he carried around with him as well as a *specific* tiny triceratops. These had to be kept track of at all times because if they were misplaced the result would possibly be the end of the world.
- Then there was the list of what to do, or where to put Ryder, if Ryder needed to be calmed down or if he started hurting himself from frustration.

When I was finished, there were *three full pages* of instructions for Ryder taped to the front of my refrigerator, and my handwriting is not large. That was The Moment of Awakening for me. I stood in front of the refrigerator just soaking up all I had written, and I thought to myself, "This is not normal."

Then I felt tremendously guilty because the pages in front of me literally helped me see how much focus was on Ryder each day. No wonder when we told the girls we were going to have another baby they were both upset with us. They couldn't love their brothers more now, but back then, the news of a possible second Ryder in the house probably made them consider running away or worse. My "neglectful mother" guilt was real.

As the due date drew closer and closer, the guilt became heavier because before each C-Section I prepare myself for death. I always prepare myself for the reality that I might not make it through the delivery which would mean this time, my girls would be burdened with the pressure of what it required for their brother to be taken care of. My guilt led me to the Dollar Tree where I picked up three tubs and filled them with games, surprises, and little toys to keep the kids busy. They had a tub of distraction to open for each day I was at the hospital. I also wrote encouraging notes to the girls pointing out their gifts, reminding them how proud I was of them and how much I loved them.

Obviously, we survived the surgery and the days away from home, and Mimi survived three days and two nights in what was equivalent to a few episodes of an extreme survival game show. She did great, but I could tell she sure was ready to be back home after I arrived back from the hospital by how quickly she kissed the kids, then bolted from the front door.

William and I were a little worried about how Ryder was going to handle our new baby, Logan. Ryder had stopped nursing over a year before Logan was born, but he still fell asleep each night with me holding him. Ryder had gotten used to being the baby and to not having to wait for me to get him what he wanted. Would Ryder be a danger to Logan because Logan was the new baby in town and my attention was going to be on another human being possibly more than it was on Ryder each day?

Yet the way in which Ryder accepted Logan was a beautiful blessing. I have to give credit where it's deserved though. The hand goes to Elmo. Yep. That's right, Elmo. Thanks to the show "Elmo's World," Ryder had watched Elmo talk to and kiss babies. When we introduced Logan as Baby Logan, Ryder gave him a kiss on the head, lightly touched his little brother's arm, and then turned to go play in his bedroom. We began to notice a bit of patience in Ryder as well. After asking for something, he would give us a *few* more seconds before getting upset because we weren't moving fast enough. (We are still working on this patience issue.)

With the introduction of Logan in the house, it was obvious that Ryder loved Baby Logan, but something else was obvious to us as well. Ryder didn't quite understand Logan's emotional cues. Most children I had been around showed some sign of distress at the cry of a baby in desperation, even if they were very young. When Baby Logan was desperate for ninny, crying that newborn cry of "Help me! They are starving me!" and I was doing my best to get to him as quick as I could, the tension in the house grew substantially. The girls and William couldn't do too much to help Logan when he was hungry since his only source of food was breastmilk. So as he cried, they were internally biting their nails off while giving me death stares, urging me to hurry up and finish whatever I was doing. Ryder, however, was casually and calmly playing off in la la land. Sometimes he would even lean over Logan and laugh at the sight of him shrieking. I think Ryder thought Logan was goofing off. Later we realized this was a red flag for autism, an inability to read emotion and facial cues well.

I clearly remember the first day I saw Ryder improve in this area. He was four and a half and I was putting on my face in my bathroom while Ryder and Baby Logan rolled around on our king-size bed. (Boys, they are always wrestling). Well, Baby Logan rolled a bit too far and rolled straight off the bed and onto the floor. It is not more than two feet from our bed to the floor, and Logan landed on carpet so he wasn't crying. But the fall did startle him and he paused there for a moment with his arms and legs splayed out beside him. Ryder hopped off the bed to attend to his brother by slightly toughing Logan's belly and asking him sweetly, "Are you ok?"

SUCCESS! IMPROVEMENT! Did he fully understand what he was saying and doing? Or was he mimicking the actions of someone else he had seen on TV? Who cares!? He knew what to say at the right time to demonstrate empathy toward his brother. The precious moment was assuring.

4

Swimming Pools and Padded Rooms

I THINK OUR SECOND CHILD, KAY, MAY GROW UP TO BE AN ARCHITECT. SHE loves to create homes and structures on Minecraft and Sims. She can't get enough of it and she creates the wildest things, such as interior greenhouses and basement pools. A free-lance architect or interior designer is a job that will suit her 'don't bore me' personality.

While we were in the car driving one day, Kay asked me what my dream home would look like and if I think she should be a judge or an architect when she grows up. (Her mind is all over the place sometimes. She gets that from me.) The conversation went on between us for the length of the hour trip since we also both like to talk, and as in most conversations in our household, autism crept into it.

We discussed the fact scientists and experts agree autism will be more prevalent in our society as the years pass which will create opportunities for people who are creative, like Kay. We started to put together our idea of a perfect home for our type of family. Kay suggested an indoor mini-pool because Ryder is a fish. A month before we were having this conversation Ryder learned how to turn the bathwater on by himself, essentially flooding the bathroom. (It took an entire king size comforter to soak all the water up from the floor.)

He has loved water since birth. At six months I remember him rolling over in the bathtub laughing and scaring me half to death. By age two, he was taking a *minimum* of six baths a day (I am seriously not exaggerating. You only thought *your* water bill was high.) We decided to purchase a small pool when he was three and then upgraded to a larger pool by the time he was four. Ryder has just turned five, and he can swim like Forest Gump can run! He swims from either side of the pool, underwater the entire time, flips and twirls like a dolphin, and dives under to the bottom to just hang out. He joins the local swim team this March. (I hope he will keep his trunks on during competition because he really doesn't like to swim with them on at home.) Swimming is one of Ryder's gifts and I consider it as a gift to us as well since we don't worry about him drowning, unlike many families who have a child on the spectrum.

I suggested a padded room for a home designed for an autism family. Not a padded room to toss the kids into, but a padded room for the adults to take a time-out. We could still use one from time to time, but we could've really used one the first few years of Ryder's life, especially the years before he was diagnosed.

Those of you who have been there know what I mean.

I have read how some parents cried, or how others pressed into God during the struggles of the early years when raising an autistic child. I certainly had my fair share of tears along the way, and what goes on between God and myself is my business. However, we didn't consider Ryder could be autistic until he was three. I didn't know *what* was going on for years, and I knew nothing of the spectrum. Because of my lack of knowledge on the subject, I am ashamed to say that for three years I started stashing bombs.

Not real bombs, of course. (The good Lord knows I don't need Homeland Security at my door.) But internally I was stashing sticks of dynamite away every time Ryder would throw a fit over a minor detail. If he wouldn't allow me to touch him when he got hurt – I would stash a bomb. We would go to the grocery store, he would get overstimulated and the pitch of his fervent screaming would have everyone staring or even approaching us with smart a** remarks – I would stash a bomb. Other parents would create posts on social media of their kid's accomplishments, kids who were the same age as Ryder, but Ryder was much further behind them – I would stash a bomb. Family vacations, playdates, church, and eating at restaurants came to a screeching halt for the fear of meltdowns – I would stash a bomb. Ryder would sneak outside without saying anything and we would catch him at the far end of the driveway – I would stash a bomb. We would listen to his unending, eyeball-curdling yowl from the backseat of the car for so long I would actually get the urge to run the car into a cement pole –lucky for us, I stashed a bomb instead. You get the point.

Then those hidden bombs would EXPLODE out of nowhere. I would never believe I could act so childish as to kick a dent into our washer or a hole into our kitchen cabinet while shrieking at the inanimate object, but I did. All of my stress, worry, fear, and guilt would build up inside and then just ERUPT. Judge me if you want, or assume you will never have moments like I have had, but you don't know how you will react until you have been in my shoes. I was grinding my teeth at night to the point I had to get a mouth guard, my hair was thinning, I was putting on extra pounds and I had a rash that would appear on the back of my neck and in the creases of my elbows. This rash itched like nothing I had ever experienced and I couldn't shake it. I am not one to visit the doctor for every little thing, but I had to make an appointment or I was going to scratch myself bloody. Doc told me I had too much stress in my life and that was the cause of the rash.

Um. Duh.

Anger would creep up on me in the strangest of places. Once we took a day-trip to the zoo. The zoo was one place we could visit where Ryder's squawks and roars didn't draw too much attention, and he enjoyed the sights long enough to give our stress levels a break. It was our tradition to ride the miniature train around the zoo before we headed home. This visit, as the train bumped and rumbled down the train tracks with us stuffed into the tiny train cars, we passed the park area just outside of the zoo, and there was a young mother enjoying a picnic with her three- or four-year-old daughter. The mother's stomach was huge and round, she looked to be at least seven months pregnant. They were so happy, smiling and laughing. I heard a voice in my head say, "You are both so happy now. You had just better pray that baby in your stomach doesn't come out being autistic because your life sure won't be so sunny anymore." I actually scared myself as I heard the horrible voice speak in my mind. The feelings I was experiencing were so unlike me.

I love all of my children and I often feel guilty for the way they saw me handle the sucker punch we were dealt because it wasn't just me experiencing the stress, and I would've liked to have been a better example by responding differently. Yes, a padded room would have been a nice escape to have a few years ago, just saying.

P.S. – If you find yourself where I was a few years ago, find an outlet! I discovered exercise is the best outlet for me. Even a short jog or some pushups in the morning can make all the difference in the day. And blasting some good music at a volume level louder than your children while dancing around your house is a great outlet for stress as well. Keeping a journal has turned into an extremely clarifying outlet for me, but if you are able to afford a padded room, go for it. You can always convert it into a closet, a panic room, or a bedroom for your dog.

5

It's a Red Blotch / No, It's an Elephant

Dawn is our oldest child, and she is our artist. She plays piano, and she has always been the one in the family who received art supplies for Christmas because everyone knew she would use them. So she took a small canvas one day and melted a bunch of crayons all over it using a blow dryer. It's a masterpiece of modern art and the canvas is placed on our wall in our home where we can all admire it.

Ryder sees an elephant on this canvas where I see a red blotch. Every time the canvas grabs his attention, he points out the red elephant. I mess with him and tell him, "It's a red blotch." Ryder will *always* correct me and say, "No, isa elephant." The truth is it is both a red blotch and an elephant of course. Ryder and I just view the red area on the canvas differently.

The difference in how we see the canvas is a good example of how Ryder's autism works at its most basic level. There are other social and communicative challenges Ryder experiences, but his senses are his foundation and he sees and experiences things differently than we do. His senses of smell, taste, touch, hearing, and sight are all functioning at different levels than yours and mine. This difference in senses makes him special. However, it can also make him highly anxious or frustrated and that can lead to an animalistic fit of howling, clawing, and kicking.

Many people have described what autism is like from a child's point of view and in my opinion, Ryder's current occupational therapist has done the best job of it. She describes Ryder as being born into an alien world, or in other words, into a world that he is not made for, so he has to learn how to adjust to it. Ryder will need to adjust to life on earth similarly to how a young Superman had to learn to adjust.

In the comics, Superman had the ability to see through walls, fly, hear conversations around the world, and a bunch of other natural-born abilities which he had to figure out how to control (as he grew up on an alien planet) so he could productively function in everyday society. Ryder will have to learn how to control some of his natural-born sensory issues in order to live an independent life as an adult. I am not Ryder, so I don't know one hundred percent of what is going on with his senses, but because I am his mother and half of him is genetically me, I am the next best thing to him telling you himself just how different his senses are, based on what I have witnessed. So here I go:

Smell. I know he smells far better than most humans, and strong smells are a big issue for him. We adopted some puppies from the local SPCA a few years ago. The moment we stepped into the holding area for the dogs and the main door closed, Ryder started to gag and then vomit from the smell of the kennel. The mixture of dog breath, dog urine, and dog feces is a pretty strong smell for all of us, but we could handle it long enough to browse the kennels. Not Ryder. He had to wait outside in the car while we picked out our new pets.

Ryder can smell the difference between different brands of food too, and one time his sense of smell left us gapped mouthed and speechless. Ryder loves Hershey's chocolate; he won't eat any other kind. We were concerned about cavities at one point because he wanted so much chocolate. We bought some sugar-free Hershey's chocolate and tasted it before offering it to him. Not only did it look identical to the regular Hershey's bar, but it also tasted the same—or so we thought. We handed Ryder an unwrapped, sugar-free, candy bar, as well as a regular candy bar and waited. We were excited because we thought we had found a way to save us from the future cost of fixing cavities and Ryder from future pain. Ryder smelled each Hershey's bar and declined the sugar-free chocolate bar. He SMELLED the difference. That blew us away.

Chapter 5—It's a Red Blotch / No, It's an Elephant

Hearing. When he wasn't speaking by a certain age or responding when we called his name, we considered that he may have a hearing problem, and we scheduled a hearing test. With the hearing test approaching, we would sit behind him at a distance of at least a yard and whisper words to see if he responded. He may not have acknowledged us when we whispered his name, but if we slightly whispered "dinosaur" or "splish-splash" Ryder would turn to look behind him. Talk about selective hearing! We already knew what the results of the hearing test would be before it was administered. His hearing is fine.

Even though he is the loudest person I have ever known, and he can hit a pitch high enough to hurt your ears, noises such as the vacuum, gun shots, or dishes crashing to the ground cause Ryder to hold his ears and run anywhere to safety. This seemed like kind of a bummer because we live in the South where hunting is a rite of passage into manhood. My husband lives to hunt year-round and would love to pass his passion for hunting with guns down to Ryder, but gunfire is way too much for Ryder. If Ryder even *sees* a gun, he takes off running. Fortunately, my husband's other big hobby is fishing, and Ryder loves fishing, or anything else to do with water, so Ryder will complete his rite of passage into manhood as my husband's fishing buddy instead.

Taste. Picky doesn't even begin to describe Ryder's sense of taste. Even though he was nursed until he was fifteen months old, and we have introduced many healthy foods to him, his eating habits are ridiculously limited. If we sing to him about Mac N Cheese versus just putting it in front of him, he is more likely to try the Mac N Cheese. He used to eat apples and bananas because of that funny little song which changes the vowels up to make the words sound silly, but he only eats peeled apples now and shoves bananas in our face to watch us eat them. He doesn't drink milk, but he loves chocolate ice cream. He likes farm fresh eggs from our chickens, but only if they are cut into Mickey Mouse ears by a cookie cutter. He really likes McDonald's fries. He likes them too much. Ryder would *live* off of McDonald's fries if we let him. We have tried to cook them at home exactly like McDonald's does or buy fries from another fast food establishment (because the entire family is so sick of McDonald's) and put those fries into a McDonald's fry container, but Ryder can tell the difference.

With all of his strange and picky eating habits, we were naturally concerned about the amount of vitamins and minerals he was missing out on. I had begun to read up a little on fermented cod liver oil when I was concerned about Ryder's teeth and when I got to the page of the book which had a chart that compared fermented cod liver oil to other foods, I closed the book. I made a decision that I had to get the stuff, and *somehow* I had to get Ryder to eat it. A tablespoon of fermented cod liver oil provides a huge amount of health to picky eater's bodies, a simple tablespoon. I purchased the plain fermented cod liver oil, and I could've slapped myself across the face when it came in the mail. It's fishy smell and flavor was over-powering. I almost gagged smelling it. *Why* did I not order the highly reviewed cinnamon flavored oil? I knew there was no *way* I was getting Ryder to eat the stuff without holding him down and force feeding it to him. Or so I thought. I was cooking good old beef-flavored ramen noodles one day. (I know ramen is unhealthy, but I will feed Ryder anything just to see him eat something.) I added a tablespoon of the fermented cod liver oil to the beef ramen noodles and passed the bowl to Ryder. I braced myself for a bit of noise and possible dish throwing. But the physical opposition never happened. He did notice the difference in the smell and the taste of the ramen, but he ate it! Then angels descended from heaven, and we all began to sing, "Hallelujah!"

Touch. His sense of touch is the sense we really have to work on. It's why he doesn't like clothes. I don't know if the feeling of the clothes actually hurts him or just irritates him, but he despises clothes. We have tried different kinds of materials as far as fabric goes, but he still prefers to be nude. His sensitivity to touch is why he likes swimming so much. Ryder's therapist told us how the pressure of the water with the feel of it against his skin is soothing for him and the feeling of weightlessness calms him. Being in water makes Ryder feel the way we would feel after a day at the spa.

Touch truly is a peculiar thing with Ryder because while he has a sensitivity to clothing, he isn't entirely opposed to people touching him. Ryder loves to be loved. He has always loved "squeezy hugs" from mommy and "tickle kisses" from daddy. He loves his weighted blanket or digging under a large pile of laundry still warm from the dryer, but heaven forbid we put clothes on him!

Sight. Ryder's sense of sight isn't spectacular enough to make him an X-man, but it isn't too shabby. He has a great eye for detail and can spot things quickly from far off. His good eyesight makes it extra hard to dodge any place Ryder wants to go if he sees it out of the car window.

Chapter 5—It's a Red Blotch / No, It's an Elephant

Bright lights tend to get him excited, while dim lighting can help to calm him down.

Colors have an impact on Ryder too. There are certain colors which make him giddy when they are grouped together such as green with purple or red with blue. Our board game collection is missing any pawn that is green, purple, red, or blue, since Ryder swipes them the moment the game is initially opened. We actually have a small tin can full of tiny items we have collected to use in place of missing game pawns Ryder has appropriated. It makes for some interesting games. Would you rather play the game as the Eraser or the Earring?

Those extras. Ryder's autism comes with one more sensory issue and as with most things on the spectrum it is custom-tailored to his individual case. A.K.A Sensory Processing Disorder. May I introduce you to the PVT&I (Proprioceptive, Vestibular, Tactile, and Interoception) Systems? You see, we all have more senses other than the basic five we are taught in grade school.

Ryder's Proprioceptive System (muscles and joints) works better after he has done some heavy lifting or serious trampoline jumping.

Ryder's Vestibular System (balance and orientation) works better after he has swung back and forth like a circus trapeze artist.

Ryder's Tactile System ties into his sense of taste is why he is such a picky eater. It is also a major factor as to why keeping him clothed is extremely challenging.

The Interoception System is an interesting one. With Ryder's Interoception System he has a higher tolerance for certain pains, a lower tolerance for others, and the kiddo has a difficult time recognizing when he is hungry. He has hunger pains, but he doesn't quite realize why.

And all of these sensory systems need to be worked with *daily*, in a *specific* order developed to help Ryder's body and mind work well together.

Heavy stuff, I know.

Energy. Then there is *The Force*. Ryder is really good at sensing the energy in a room or the energy coming from a person. Even when he was tiny, maybe eight months old, I remember telling a wise, older lady friend how strange it was that Ryder was so calm with Mimi when we would visit her on holidays or weekends. It seemed he could sense something special about Mimi. This natural acceptance of Mimi stood out to me because Ryder was around a lot of the same people for the first year of his life, but Ryder wouldn't be agreeable for anyone besides my husband and me. My older lady friend told me, "Some babies can sense real emotion, and they just know when someone loves them." I agree. Ryder can *feel* when we are exasperated with him. We have learned it is better to leave the room until we calm down before the energy we are generating causes a bigger problem.

The same thing goes for when we are very proud of him. He eats up the positive energy. He gives us at least two "high-fives," his grin grows two sizes bigger, then he squeals with delight. If I could just bottle up that squeal of delight, I could sell it as a homeopathic energy drink, helping to fight addiction to anti-depressants.

6

Acknowledgement

THE WINDOWS AND CURTAINS TO MY BEDROOM WERE OPEN THIS MORNING, letting in a refreshing breeze and just the right amount of sunshine to wake me up slowly. Spring is my favorite season in Texas. As I unsealed my eyes and watched the chickens peck around in the front yard, I flashed back to another window I used to look out of regularly where we were living when Ryder was a young toddler. From the large kitchen windows of the old house, we could see the span of the property. The view was breathtaking. The pond was just down the hill from the house. Beyond the pond were acres and acres of pastureland surrounded by woods. The sky went on forever.

I think writing this little book of raw truths has triggered memories which I had wanted to forget. This morning, watching the chickens through my bedroom window, I remembered the day I was sitting at the kitchen table with Dawn working on her math lesson, and looking through those kitchen widows. It was the day we discovered Ryder was a "quiet bolter."

Ryder was happily playing in the dirt beneath the swing set just beyond the open kitchen window. He would usually play there fascinated with the dirt longer than most kids could. Dawn and I were both checking to make sure he was ok between math problems. Then, in the time it took us to finish one fraction problem, Ryder was gone. Immediately, we jumped up and ran outside to search for him. The idea that he had gotten very far seemed silly. Dawn has always been pretty quick with math so we had only looked away for a minute at the most! Our house was on a hill so we could see for long distances around the house, yet the grass of the rolling pasture land was higher than regular grass. We first considered that he could be lying down in the grass close to the house like the kids did while playing hide and seek, or he could've decided to toddle off toward the chicken coop to find eggs, which was also close to our house. Nope. Ryder had decided to head to the pond.

The pond was at least 100 yards away from the house, and he had never attempted to go there by himself before. He had taken a route to the pond by the side of the house along a fence line where we couldn't see him from the kitchen window. We must have just missed him as we ran outside. If he had decided to head to the pond straight down the hill instead of to the side, we would've caught him in no time. Still he must have been booking it to make it to the pond so quickly.

Dawn had jumped on the ATV while I was running around like a chicken with its head cut off. After searching for over two minutes, (which was actually two days in frantic-parent-time), Dawn found him by the shallower end of the pond. He had his feet in the water already. He was wearing his brown and orange stripped zip-up sleeper, and ants were starting to crawl up his pajama pant legs. He was only two years old at the time, and he could not swim. If Dawn had not found Ryder when she did, he would've died. I am certain that would've been the last morning we would have had with him.

I was only a few months along in my pregnancy with Logan, and I knew that I wouldn't be able to move quickly enough to save Ryder from drowning when I was huge in another few months. So that day I put up the ugliest fence imaginable around our house. William was working an extra-long hitch so I had to construct something to contain Ryder on my own, using material that was easy enough for me to quickly set up. The ugly fence was made of green metal stakes and white plastic lattice secured in place by multi-colored zip-ties. Who cared what it looked like? Its sole purpose was to contain Ryder and keep him alive. William came home about a week later, stepped out of his truck, and stopped dead in his tracks. As he stared ahead he asked, "What did you do?"

The ugly fence did its job. Ryder is still with us.

Dawn is such a huge help when it comes to Ryder's care. I need to acknowledge her because she really pulled through for us in the early years. William's work would keep him away for weeks at a time so a lot of responsibility fell on our oldest child.

When Ryder was a 'bolter' and a 'screamer,' Dawn would ride along with me to run errands without ever getting to come inside the store or the bank or wherever we needed to go. She was twelve or thirteen and made the best of the torture by taking selfies of her smiling with an upset Ryder in his car seat in the background. She was much more patient than I was in many situations. If Ryder's behavior came to a point where I had to leave the room, Dawn would step in to calm Ryder down and get him what he needed. She was the one who discovered the phrase which calmed Ryder down almost immediately, a tender "It will be ok." She tended to Ryder when we were in the car and I couldn't reach behind me to get his cup or change the video he was watching. This was stressful for Dawn since Ryder has never had any amount of patience. When we would visit friends, she would take Ryder for lengths at a time so that I could sit long enough to have a cup of coffee with our hostess. When Ryder wanted to hang out with Dawn and her friends, she would include him even though her friends weren't too pleased with it, and I am sure she wasn't always thrilled.

When Logan was born and I was pleading with God to either give me four arms or a robot nanny, Dawn saved the day too many times to count. Thanks to her I was able to actually shower and cook dinner from time to time.

When I was her age, I probably would've jumped ship, but Dawn chose to help and she has even mentioned working within the autistic community as a career after college.

The world needs more Dawns.

Our next door neighbor would comment on what a wonderful big sister she was, and I would always add to their comment, "Dawn has saved Ryder's life too many times to count. He wouldn't be here without her."

Part II

DIGGING IN

Death, Taxes, and Autism

I KNEW NOTHING ABOUT AUTISM BEFORE RYDER WAS DIAGNOSED OTHER than what I had seen in the movie *Rain Man*. I didn't even know Asperger's and autism were on the same spectrum or that an autism spectrum even existed. If autism hadn't crashed into our lives, I probably would've seen a child acting out like Ryder does and be the person to assume he was spoiled. We had Ryder tested because we could see he was different from other children, and once the final diagnosis was made, our suspicions were confirmed, and we were going in a new direction, we naturally started to look for a *cure*. In the back of my mind I was thinking, "Whatever the cure costs, we will pay for it. If we have to drive across the country to get the cure, we will go. We are going to fix this."

I continued to read everything I could get my hands on about autism and how to fix Ryder. I was bombarded with the many "remedies" for autism, and we tried any remedies which other parents claimed had cured their child of autism or at least lessened the symptoms.

Let's see, we fed Ryder a detox clay that claimed to remove heavy metals from his system and cure autism. That didn't work. (But the clay makes for an *awesome* facial mask!)

We purchased some fancy essential oils to diffuse in the house and rub on Ryder. All that did was make our place stink like a head shop and bring about a huge protest from Ryder since he dislikes *any* kind of lotion, oil, or ointment touching him.

I went crazy on Amazon Prime and ordered an entire pantry filled with gluten-free foods. When the shipment arrived, I thought I would try some of it myself before we started the rave diet of the decade for autistics. The food was disgusting! Most of the stuff I had ordered which was gluten-free was so packed with sugar as the main ingredient that the food was actually gritty. I thought, "Sure this stuff might help with autism, but it will also give your kid diabetes." I called a friend whose daughter has celiac disease and she was more than happy to accept the pantry full of food.

The more I read and the more remedies we tried, the more I realized that there is no cure for autism. Ryder's brain formed differently in the womb. He did not contract autism, and autism is not a cancer spreading inside him. He IS autistic.

Once I finally let this sink in, I could look back and see all the red flags we missed from the day Ryder was born to the day he was diagnosed.

The very first night in the hospital after Ryder was born the nurses were checking on us more frequently than usual because Ryder was constantly crying. Not just crying, screaming to the point that the other patients in the hospital were calling the nurses because they were concerned. Ryder was nursing well and he was very healthy, but unless he was wrapped snuggly in my arms or nursing, he was wailing and it took him a while to calm down once he got started. I would finally get him subdued, then a nurse would come into the room to check vitals, lights would need to be turned on, Ryder would get disturbed, so he would want to nurse, then he would poo and I would have to change him by unwrapping him from his blanket, then the wailing would start all over again. It was like he was a vampire being exposed to sunlight, the outer world was *painful*.

The second night we were in the hospital after Ryder's birth was the worst. He had been circumcised that morning so the noise was extreme after a diaper change. That night when the nurse came in to ask if he was receiving enough breastmilk because the woman in the room next door was concerned about my baby (again), I told her, "This is my third child I have nursed, he is *not*

Chapter 7—Death, Taxes, and Autism

hungry, and he does *not* need a bottle. Perhaps he is just pissed that the end of his wee-wee has been snipped off." (Hey, I had been sliced open, I was on heavy medication, and I was tired. They simply had to forgive my rudeness.) That was a really long hospital visit.

As he grew, Ryder had a delay in speaking, but he was our first boy and we were told by nearly every mother of a boy that boys usually speak later than girls so we didn't think much about it. Four years of his life went by so quickly, we didn't realize until he began taking speech therapy how far behind in language Ryder really was. We had become accustomed to his language of grunts and sounds to the point that we understood him without his using words.

He was perfectly fine playing in his room by himself for hours, lining up his little toys, stacking blocks, or watching DVDs. On nice weather days Ryder would sit outside in the dirt or in the little pool, happily entertaining himself for long periods of time. If we had friends come over to visit and the house was full of people, Ryder would insist on sitting in my car and watching TV until our company was gone. We figured he simply wasn't a social butterfly and we didn't dare question the rare moments when he was completely content and not upset at the world.

Ryder did the coolest things at an early age like lining up the ABCs in order or creating patterns with shapes and memorizing dances. We knew our son was super gifted but didn't connect these gifts to autistic traits. There were lots of other red flags we should have seen but we didn't.

We were living in a bubble until autism popped the bubble, and then I started thinking of the parents I knew who had children with cerebral palsy or peanut allergies. My eyes were suddenly wide open and I was amazed by how well they functioned daily with their children's struggles. You never really know how much of a fight it takes to raise a disabled child, until your own child is fighting against a handicap they will live with for the rest of their life.

I've always tried to embrace how we are all different and how our differences make this planet of humans fascinating. The Conscious Me is at terms with autism, but dog-nab-it, I occasionally still find Subconscious Me asking, "Why is Ryder autistic? Did I do something during my pregnancy to cause his autism? Did we smoke some laced marijuana in high school and it stayed in my system? Is there someone in my family lineage who is autistic that I don't know about? Is his autism caused by the chemicals in our food or the vaccines we receive? Were we unknowingly part of some government experiment during my pregnancy?"

There are many theories and speculations on where autism stems from, what causes it, and what may trigger it. We can look back and see Ryder's autism since birth, which really makes us believe Ryder's autism is genetic or environmental, but other parents claim vaccines triggered autism in their children or that their child was just fine until a certain age and then their child began to lose his speech and eventually regressed into autism. Perhaps all of the above are reasons for the rise in autism. (Well, except for the government experiment theory.)

Autism has been the single most frustrating thing I have obsessed over in the past five years. Autism creeps into everything, you can't get away from it. Every conversation we have will eventually turn toward autism or autism will at least be mentioned. Every place we go we have to consider how autism will either make or break the day. Functional clothes, tennis shoes, my hair in a ponytail, and a purse that is worn across my chest, help me feel I have more control in case of a meltdown, so it's a good thing I have never been a 'skirt and heels' type of gal. When we watch movies that used to make us laugh, such as *Waterboy*, I now get angry at the portrayal of a neurologically different person being made fun of by others. When we talk about retirement or our children's futures, our concerns over Ryder's independence always surface. With every mention of war or financial ruin mentioned in the news, I secretly plot and plan about how to care for Ryder in a post-apocalyptic environment. You see, I know the steel building not too far from our house is a Frito-Lay potato chip storage and transfer facility. I have actually had the thought that in the event of a true extended, fight-for-survival type of emergency, I could find chips for Ryder at that steel building to keep him calm. (Raising autism can make you consider the most bizarre scenarios.)

When Logan was a tiny newborn, I read a statistic that really had me shaking in my fuzzy house shoes. The statistic showed it is very common for a sibling of an autistic to be autistic too, especially if the sibling is male and born within 2-3 years of their autistic brother. "Yee Haw!" I thought. Life was already *so* wild with one autistic son, the child in my arms was male, and he was born with only two-and-a-half years separating him from Ryder. Phew! Life with two autistic sons? I started to measure myself for a strait jacket.

Chapter 7—Death, Taxes, and Autism

I would be a liar if I said I wasn't relieved when we realized Logan is neurotypical (what a fancy word for "normal brained.") From time to time I feel like an idiot for not seeing those early signs of autism in Ryder. Since Logan was born so closely to Ryder, the memories of Ryder's early years are fresh in my mind and I am able to compare the similarities and differences between the two boys. There was quite a bit going on with Ryder that we shrugged off to his being a boy instead of him possibly having a different neurological order. To the parents who raise more than one autistic child I say, "You deserve a medal!" and "Come on over anytime because I know you need a break, a place of acceptance, and probably some chocolate cake. My coffee pot is always on, and your children are welcome to run wild with mine."

We recently signed up for a nationwide study called SPARK (Simons Foundation Powering Autism Research for Knowledge). We sent them our personal information and DNA samples from myself, my husband, Ryder and Logan. The geneticists behind the SPARK study are searching for answers behind the rise in autism and what part genetics play into autism. I can't wait to see the results of this study because I've heard scientists predict that half of the children born in the U.S. by 2025 will have autism. My brain can't comprehend this prediction. 2025 is just around the corner! Our country is in for a big surprise. The phrase "Nothing is certain in life except death, taxes, and autism," runs through my head.

Perhaps we should focus more on how to integrate autism into our world instead of focusing on a cure or cause for autism? (First things first, right?) At least my girls will be better prepared than I was, if any of them have an autistic child, since they've had years of experience. Everything happens for a reason. Life with Ryder could be prepping my girls to be the most awesome parents.

8

Ryder Says, "Adapt"

WHEN WE WERE A NEUROTYPICAL FAMILY, I SURE DID TAKE A LOT FOR granted. As our life began to twist and turn with autism, we were forced to adapt.

Sleeping patterns have changed.

Going out in public can cause extreme anxiety for everyone in the family.

Non-immediate family members constantly voice their unwanted opinions.

Therapy and doctors' appointments have become the center of the scheduling universe.

Our household remains a one-income household even though life has become more expensive since constant supervision is required.

Providing that constant supervision can easily burn us out.

And as you have been reading, there have been many other challenges for us while raising an autistic.

Love and Marriage—Did you know the divorce rate among parents of autistic children escalates from the American average of 50 percent to a steep 80 percent? That's scary! I have been with my husband since I met him the summer I was fifteen years old, and he is still the man I am crazy for. Marriage is work though! We've had our ups and downs, and we still disagree like any other married couple over finances or life in general. But when I started suggesting to my husband that I thought our firstborn son was different from other kids, he didn't take it so well. He wasn't mad. Instead he held a stance of defense with some feelings of denial. I completely understood when he said, "There is nothing wrong with my son." I agreed with him and I didn't enjoy pointing out Ryder's differences, but I couldn't ignore what I saw every day before my own eyes while my husband was at work. There was nothing wrong with Ryder, but Ryder was *definitely* different than other children.

I was hesitant to push the subject because it was around this time that I found the statistics on divorce, and I had read horror stories from mothers who said their husbands didn't know how to react to their child's autism so they simply didn't interact with their child, sometimes for years. (Talk about something that could rip a marriage apart!) I also didn't push the subject because I was still struggling within myself, trying to figure out what the next step was.

Will was home from work for a few months when Ryder was three. He got the pleasure of experiencing what I did on a daily basis. And it was at this point in Ryder's life when William agreed there was something different about Ryder when compared to other kids his age. From there, we scheduled an evaluation.

My husband is a gem though, and he never turned away from us through the course of diagnosis and beyond. He gallantly enters Ryder's world to interact with him every day as he continues to be a wonderful father to all our children. It is not uncommon for our house to sound like a zoo because William does great animal impressions which Ryder requests from him *constantly*. And quite a few times when I have been trying to work with Ryder but it simply wasn't happening, William has thought of something brilliant to help us overcome the problem. When Ryder was showing interest in coloring, we happily obliged, but his grip on the crayons wasn't strong enough to color within the lines. Even though I was so proud of him, Ryder was a harsh critic of himself, and he wanted to crumble up and throw away every attempt at coloring. William suggested I create a handmade coloring book using a wide tipped permanent marker. This made the outer lines of the pictures big enough where Ryder could color within the lines a bit better. He was so proud of himself after only the first picture he completed, and he gave a large smile for the camera.

Retirement planning is an important part of marriage, and we have had to plan for the possibility that our autistic child may not be an independent adult. I think the recent statistic I read was that only 17 percent of autistic adults currently live outside the home. So we not only have to financially plan for our retirement, but also for an entire lifetime after our own.

Going out on date nights pretty much cease to exist. (At least, it did for us.) Last week my husband and I went out together for the first time in *five* years. I was a nervous wreck. I kept expecting my mother-in-law to call asking us to come back. After years of learning how to work with Ryder, I had a hard time releasing the reigns and letting someone else cling to them during bedtime, but everyone was alive when we returned home.

We've had to become pretty creative for any "private time" too. That comes hand-in-hand with having four children, but if anything can discourage a romantic moment more than little ones knocking on your bedroom door, it's an autistic meltdown happening on the other side of that door. So we've become creative to keep the spark alive, taking or making any opportunity for "private time" in the oddest places and moments.

Housing—Another issue we have encountered has to do with where we live. We moved to our current home not because of a job transfer, the great school district, and definitely not because everyone would finally have their own room. We moved here because it's the home directly next door to Mimi and Papa, and we needed *help*! When I say directly, I mean there is literally a path going from our yard into their yard. Thank God the ex-owner decided to kick out her non-rent paying son to sell us her home after Papa asked her the uncommon question, "Would you like to sell your house?"

I remember when my husband came to me and asked, "How does a 1999 double wide trailer on a bit of land right next to Mimi & Papa sound?" I told him it sounded like hell to most people, but considering we were currently in a type of hell already, I would be willing to try out the 1999 double wide idea. Even though we live in the South where trailers are abundant, there is still a stigma that comes with living in a trailer. Trailers are notorious for rotting out from under your feet in this humidity, they are hard to finance, tornados seem to target them, and people tend to assume you are trashy if you live in a trailer, but we had to try something.

We had different plans as far as housing was concerned when Ryder was a small baby. We were living on 32 acres of beautiful rolling pasture land with a two-acre stocked pond, stables for the animals, surrounded by woods, and nestled in a small and peaceful town. Our plans included building our dream log cabin home and raising our kids on a farm.

After all is said and done though, I am glad autism changed our place of living because there was no changing that Ryder had autism, and moving here has been the beginning of a new and more functional life for *all* of us. We now live close enough to a town where speech and occupational therapy are just a ten minute drive away, and all the kids love to spend time with Mimi or Papa whenever they want to. My personal stress level went down five notches when we moved in since I knew help was just around the corner if I needed it.

Feeding pigs and horses every day is not as fun as it sounds and that dream of a log cabin home can still happen someday since trailers are also easily demolished. Either way, we discovered it is not the type of home you live in that makes a happy family; it is a happy family that makes your house a real home.

Safety Measures—Home security takes on an entirely new meaning since we are not just trying to keep strangers out, but we are also trying to keep Ryder in. All yards and the driveway must be fenced with locked gates and the gates have to have wire fencing across the front of them so little bodies cannot squeeze through the cracks between the bars. We used to have sliding locks on our doors as well as the deadbolts, but Ryder is so strong that he pulled the sliding lock from the wall when he was frustrated with trying to open the door once, ruining both the trim and the sheetrock.

Last year Ryder became really upset, bolted from the front door, and started running down the driveway toward the busy street. My husband had left the house for a five-minute trip to the corner store so we didn't see the need to secure the gate at the end of the driveway. Of course, the moment we let our guard down is the moment autism decides to push the limits. I ran after Ryder as fast as I could, pleading for him to stop the entire time. I finally caught the little bugger and gave him a few swats on the behind while I sternly told him between gasps for oxygen how he had better not *ever* run away from me again.

The following morning, I added jogging to my daily exercise routine since having to catch Ryder caused me to see just how out of shape I had become after child number four. If Ryder was going to be a flight risk when he became over-angry, I needed to be able to catch him. It's not that Ryder tries to escape from this insane asylum regularly, but he likes to play outside a lot too. He knows how to open the deadbolt, and he will simply leave the house without

Chapter 8 —Ryder Says, "Adapt"

making a peep. He isn't aware of certain dangers such as getting smashed by a speeding vehicle or getting lost in the woods. What's to keep him from wandering if we don't have our perimeter secured?

When he does go outside to play and we call to him, he doesn't answer like the rest of the kids do. Finding Ryder outside means we step onto the porch and listen very carefully until we hear his little humming noises or laughter from the side of the house or behind the garden. We are constantly asking each other, "Where is Ryder? Have you seen Ryder?" It might be less stressful if we had a top-of-the-line security system allowing us to view each nook and cranny of the house from any angle. Although chances are with these boys, the system would be broken beyond repair in no time flat. So we depend on each other and we are thankful for our squeaky storm doors. Any other person would immediately hear our doors great need for some WD 40. We appreciate the fact our squeaky doors let us know when someone is coming or going.

Racket—There is much more noise here than the average family of six plus a dog. Before Ryder could speak, we would carry earplugs in the car with us in case anyone couldn't handle the volume level. One of the funniest things my husband has ever said to me on the way home from shopping was, "Hurry up and get there. I would rather do two tours in Afghanistan than sit in this car with Ryder screaming."

Once our neighbor drove over on his four-wheeler to ask me if Ryder was okay because he had heard him screaming from three acres away. I had to thank him for his concern and then explain that Ryder was just upset because he didn't want to get in the car to leave. Heaven only knows what our current neighbors assume is going on over here. They must think we are breeding chimpanzees or training a terrorist organization and lock their doors extra tight at night.

Apparel—To the uninformed eye, it might look like we are running a nudist colony. Ryder has had a problem with clothing since birth and he is naked at home 98 percent of the time. It is not only Ryder, but Logan is also naked about 80 percent of the time because he likes to copy his big brother. The only good thing about their constant nudity is a slack on the amount of laundry I have to wash. Up until Ryder was three, we were able to stockpile footed onesies with the zipper and snap button in the front, but then he figured out how to escape from them. So I found some swimwear that zipped up the back, we stockpiled those, and those worked until he grew out of them. To my huge disappointment, I can no longer find them past a size 4T. (If you are a seamstress, you could make a *fortune* starting a clothing line for autistic children and adults who do not like to wear clothes). Zippers in the back were the only thing that kept Ryder clothed from age three to four. Being naked is just not accepted in our society and we can't live on the beaches of France, so I've given up on trying to keep clothes on Ryder while he is at home. It is his home after all; I want him to be comfortable *somewhere.*

This past Christmas we had some last-minute guests from Sicily arrive with my sister and brother in law. We had a great time eating good food, drinking wine, and playing board games. Our house was full, the fireplace was blazing, and the kids had completely trashed the house with all their Christmas gifts and wrapping paper. It was a fantastic Christmas. I was so caught up in the merriness of it all that I forgot to explain Ryder's nakedness to our guests, who spoke very little English.

"Oh my goodness," I said over the phone to my sister after everyone had left. "Did you get a chance to tell them Ryder is autistic? Or were they totally perplexed over the little naked boy running around?"

"I think my husband mentioned something to them," she replied, and we both laughed.

If Ryder wants something from us, however, we tell him he has to have underwear on before he will get it. Ryder will comply with that request three-out-of-five times, but then he strips back down to nothing when we're not looking. This past fall my husband was cleaning up the yard and he came into the house with four pairs of dirty underwear in his hands. He had found these *Paw Patrol* underwear stashed throughout the property. I told him, "That explains all the missing underwear, and you can't say I don't try to keep clothes on him."

We brush his body with a body brush before dressing him for outings to help with his sensitivity to clothing. Hopefully, he will grow out of this sensitivity. Thank goodness he has only tried to get naked three times in public. If you are coming to visit us, we will try to remember to warn you that our oldest boy is running bare. If you happen to visit us unannounced, like the carpet cleaning people did a few months back, you are going to see Ryder in his birthday suit. That's pretty much all I can say about that.

9

Ryder Says, "Hold on Tight"

ALMOST EVERY AVERAGE DAILY TASK IS SO GOSH DARN DIFFICULT FOR US. Things can escalate to *Def-Con crazy* in milliseconds with autism in the mix. We have simply had to hold on tight!

Oral Hygiene—Brushing Ryder's teeth is similar to what it would be like if Jane Goodall attempted to brush a silverback gorilla's teeth. For years to brush his teeth I had to either sit on Ryder or hold his hands above his head. Dental check-ups? HAH! That silverback gorilla turns into King Kong! Tranquilizers must be used—the injections, not the little banana-flavored drink. I am not kidding. Ryder's teeth are pretty strong and good looking, but he likes to chew on anything foam. Pool noodles, nun-chucks, yoga mats, and memory foam pillows don't stand a chance at our house. When he was three, some foam was stuck between his teeth that I couldn't get out. It eventually became a few bad cavities.

We found a dentist over an hour away who had experience with autistic children. They had weighted blankets and dark rooms on hand, but Ryder wasn't having it. I didn't know how I was going to get him to swallow the banana-flavored drink that he needed in order for the dentist to get his teeth fixed and the foam out. After sitting in the room with him screaming, squirming, and crying for what seemed like forever, the dental assistant came in and asked me if I would be okay with Ryder receiving an injection instead of having to drink the medicine that took forty-five minutes to knock him out. I am no idiot. I said, "Yes. Where do I sign?" Once signatures were done, they entered the room, and I held Ryder on my lap. They injected the liquid into his shoulder, we counted to ten and, BAM, Ryder was out cold and ready for dental work. I was thinking, "What was that stuff, and how do I find more?"

Hairdo—Cutting Ryder's hair is slightly worse than brushing his teeth. The task requires serious teamwork. Ryder has thick, straight hair and an awesome cowlick. As his hair grows out, it begins to look similar to Rod Stewart's hairdo. Because haircuts are such a dramatic event, we wait as long as we can between them. When Ryder begins to resemble an 80's heavy-metal rock star, my husband and I prep the bathroom as if for a surgical procedure.

Gloves? Check.

Towels? Check.

Clippers? Check.

Mouthpiece? Check.

Reward toy? Check.

I hold Ryder in my arms, tummy to tummy, and sit on the counter top while William does his best barber work. Ryders struggles and cries out. It takes a lot of work and willpower to hold him still. Once the procedure is complete, both Ryder and I are covered in hair. That is the worst part. I know how itchy I am after a haircut. Poor Ryder must feel like a thousand knives are cutting him. We really hate doing it, and we get him to the bathtub as quick as possible afterward.

Family Portraits—The suggestion of a family picture is absurd. I completely threw in the towel this year. In previous years, our family photo is full of tears and frustration. Ryder is reaching out for whoever is taking the picture to save him, sixteen-year-old Dawn has purposefully dressed in dark colors and is pleading with her eyes to disappear. Eight-year-old Kay strikes her "selfie pose," and two-year-old Logan is scowling with disapproval. All the while, my husband and I continue to smile straight ahead unflinchingly, frozen solid, with fake smiles on, not wanting to miss the precious moment the camera might capture the family *all* looking forward at the same moment.

Chapter 9 – Ryder Says, "Hold on Tight"

Since we didn't have a jacked-up family photo to slap onto our Christmas cards this year, I started to photoshop a homemade card together. It looked like a serial killer's ransom note, but with pictures instead of letters. We were all doing and wearing different things. There was no piecing it together nicely. William was driving his truck, Kay was climbing a rope, I was cooking in my pajamas, Ryder was sitting in his underwear, Dawn was—well, actually the picture of Dawn was the only normal one I could find, but they still didn't work together well. We mailed some common, but decent Christmas cards to everyone instead.

Cost and Supply —What would you say to a doctor if they suggested your child could benefit from the top-rated therapy to date (A.B.A), but it was going to cost an average of $10,000 per *month* and Medicaid as well as most private health insurance wouldn't cover it? My response was, "You're joking, right?" My husband works his butt off, and we are like any other family trying to keep the bills low and the bank account balance decent. The types of therapy close to home (speech and occupational, not ABA) only accept Medicaid or self-pay clients. Since William makes too much money for our household to qualify for Medicaid or Social Security Disability, we were having to pay for Ryder's therapy out of pocket, a mind-boggling amount of over $70.00 per *half hour*. (Paying the mortgage for a second house on the beachfront would've cost us less.)

Ryder was only getting the bare minimum of professional therapy outside of the home for months, and we started playing the lottery again, hoping to become millionaires in order to pay for more. The therapists would give us a rundown of what Ryder needed to work on, and I would Pinterest my eyeballs out to complete more therapy at home. But Texas pulled through for us, and we were eventually told of a new program called the Medicaid Buy-In Program for Children with Disabilities. Basically, we pay Medicaid a premium for Ryder to be on a Medicaid healthcare plan. In return, Ryder is able to receive any service which accepts Medicaid. We now pay a fraction of what we were paying out-of-pocket for Ryder to receive four times more therapy than he did before.

This program has helped us enormously, but the ridiculously expensive top-rated therapy Texas Children's Hospital recommended to us is still not available to disability Medicaid recipients. What kind of system are we paying taxes into when the best therapies for disabled children are so difficult to come by? What could this therapy possibly consist of for it to be $10,000 a month? Brain surgery or space exploration?

Autism is expensive not just from the cost of the therapy, but also because of what it costs to keep your sanity on a daily basis. When we finally find something Ryder will eat, we buy it in super-bulk. When the last hurricane came through, we *thought* we were prepared. We had stockpiled enough of his favorite chips to see us through Armageddon. Unfortunately, we underestimated how the amount of rain that arrived with Hurricane Harvey would directly affect us. I remember thinking that the company which made the chips must be underwater because we couldn't find these chips at any store! Weeks after the destructive waters dissipated, I came across the chips at a gas station. I dove toward the rack like a Black Friday shopper, grabbing as many as I could hold, ignoring the strange looks I received. We needed those chips!

When Ryder obsesses over a certain movie or toy, we buy at least two in case the first one turns up MIA or gets mistreated to the point of not functioning properly. We learned early on not to donate or sell any of Ryder's toys or games that happen to survive. We have tubs of his collections and toys stacked in the closet. While Ryder may not play with them every day, when he does eventually request a toy set he played with a year ago, we had better be able to produce it, or else.

I struggle with the towers of tubs and toys stacked to the ceiling. First of all, it's probably a fire hazard. Second of all, I am an organized minimalist at heart, and I secretly long for the day I can swing open our gates and have the biggest yard sale *ever*!

Blood & Pain—Thank the good Lord that Ryder hasn't had a broken bone or terrible gash. If he gets a boo-boo, even the smallest one, we cannot come near him. Heaven help us when his boo-boo is bleeding. It's a really good thing Ryder is a boy. I am clueless as to how I would approach explaining a menstrual cycle to an autistic girl if she was as scared of blood as much as Ryder.

I thought he sliced his entire finger off not too long ago because of how severe his reaction was over a bloodied cut on his finger. I had opened a can of beans for dinner but didn't take the lid completely off. I left the edge of the lid attached to the can so I could tuck the lid into the can with the idea that no one would cut themselves when the trash was being taken out. For whatever *insane* reason, when I turned my back, Ryder reached up and snatched the

Chapter 9 — Ryder Says, "Hold on Tight"

can off the counter, then stuck his finger into the can trying to pry the lid up! (I flinch just recalling the bloody incident.) He could've lost a finger! I still don't know how he got away with such a small slice, but like a razor cut when you are shaving your legs, his finger would not stop bleeding, and I imagine it burned terribly. He ran around the house screeching in pain while holding his finger. Blood was dripping from his cut through his clinched fist. All I could do was chase him while trying not to freak him out any more than he already was. When I finally caught him and was able to see that the cut wasn't as bad as we suspected, we were both so upset, I just sat him down and held back tears while he cried in my lap.

We will have to knock him out cold if he ever gets really hurt and has to go to the hospital. Unfortunately, there are a million and one reasons a child in our neck of the woods might need emergency room attention.

One of the scariest reasons is snakes.

Poisonous snakes in a Texas summer are a real threat, and snake bites have been one of my biggest fears when it comes to Ryder because the poison from a snake bite spreads rapidly if your heart rate picks up, and his heart rate would *sky rocket*. We have been working on teaching Ryder to run away if he sees a snake since before we even knew if he understood what we were saying. This summer all our repetition paid off.

Some trees needed to be cut down to make room for a future workshop. While the logs were freshly cut, the boys were enjoying walking back and forth across them. We cut down four or five trees at once, so we didn't get them chopped up or moved over that weekend. (As a matter of fact, there is still one more tree out there that needs chopping.) The boys would run outside to play on their "bridges" all summer long. I would always holler "Watch out for snakes!" as they sprinted across the yard.

One morning, Ryder was out front playing, and he came inside to tell me, "Snake," in a very serious tone. We told him to show us where the snake was. He took us over to the logs and pointed with sure confidence at a clear area between two of them, but there was no snake. It is not in Ryder's nature to make up stories or exaggerate the truth, so we kept hunting. I asked him what color the snake was. He said, "Orange." Sure enough, when we rolled over one of the logs closest to where Ryder had told us he saw a snake, there was an orange slithering serpent. I couldn't have been prouder of him.

Autism has turned our lives inside out and upside down. Many things are harder than they should be. Things don't always get better, but nothing stays the same. Changes happen, some of them accelerate toward our goals, and some are regressive. I try to keep a positive attitude by purposefully seeking and finding accomplishments in every day moments, even if they are tiny.

Today I am thankful we only had to drive to therapy, McDonald's wasn't out of fries, Ryder didn't hurt himself, the kids are all safe under our roof, and my husband and I can have a glass of wine (or maybe two) before bed.

10

It's BROKEN!

A BOARD THE CRUISE SHIP S.S. AUTISM WE OCCASIONALLY DISCOVER LITTLE islands of information, and we exclaim, "Oh! That's why Ryder does that!"

One of these is the Island of Stimming.

Stimming defined is "a repetitive body movement that self-stimulates one or more senses in a regulated manner."

When we discovered there was a convenient name for the baffling movements Ryder made or repeated, we were able to put those actions into an invisible treasure chest. Ryder will occasionally flap his hands uncontrollably. He also makes his hands swim past his face and enjoys creating the same motion with string in the wind or stuffed animal's tails. It is the "wave" motion that draws him in.

Then there is his adorable "chicken wing squeeze." When Ryder is super excited over something or extremely happy, he puts his hands under his armpits and squeals with delight while squeezing down his hands. When he does this, it seems that his happiness is too great for him to contain. His laughter while doing the "chicken wing squeeze" is contagious. I love it.

The Island of Echo has been a fun one. Ryder was three when we first noticed his echo. It had us really scratching our heads because Ryder could speak words, but not his own. Doesn't that just *sound* confusing? It was. He began copying everything we said, yet he wasn't able to independently tell us what he wanted, what was wrong, or anything else beyond "dinosaur," the ABCs, shapes, farm animals, and some foods. Then we learned about *echolalia*.

Echolalia is defined as "meaningless repetition of another person's spoken words as a symptom of psychiatric disorder."

We sure did have to be careful what we said around Ryder from there on out. If I were to get frustrated to the point of cussing, there was a small voice behind me repeating my exact words, and that small voice was *not* my conscience.

I am going to be a bit snarky here and mention how the word "meaningless" is used to define echolalia, but I don't back that up 100 percent. We make his echo work for us, giving his echo meaning. For example, we can get Ryder to tell us he loves us anytime we selfishly want to hear it. All we have to do is say it to him first. Although he shows us in many other ways that he loves us, it is very nice to hear him actually say it. As we set new speech goals and work at reaching them. If I say what he needs to learn, and he repeats it, then I at least know that he has heard me.

Ryder uses a spin-off of echolalia on us as a form of communication too. If he sees a candy, toy, or place he desires he will repeat the item, place, or activity, over and over and over *and over* again until we give him what he wants or we are able to successfully redirect his attention to something else. (It's not annoying at *all*.)

When he is really interested in something and he wants us to acknowledge him, he will repeat himself while looking at us and not stop until we copy what he is saying.

"Giraffe. Giraffe," he will repeat while standing next to me as I am trying to talk to William on the phone. I see him standing next to me holding a toy giraffe. I smile and nod at him, but continue to talk on the phone.

"Giraffe. Giraffe. Giraffe," Ryder continues repeating to me, getting really close to my ear.

I pause my phone conversation for a moment to confirm, "Yes Ryder, Giraffe. That is a very nice giraffe."

Then Ryder smiles a huge smile, takes his giraffe, and goes back to the table to play.

Chapter 10—It's BROKEN!

Yes, the cruise ship S.S. Autism can be a beautiful wondrous cruise, but we have learned to do our best to steer clear of certain "icebergs." These icebergs are part of the reason professionals have said parents of autistics can suffer from the same stress levels as soldiers in battle, even having PTSD. Imagine re-living the dramatic horror of the sinking Titanic every day because the ship is continually smashing into icebergs.

It's no wonder some of us are a nervous wreck.

The Iceberg of Completing Things has been an interesting one. When Ryder begins something, he *must* complete it. I am not only talking about common everyday things such as coloring a page or building a castle out of blocks. His need to complete is extreme. We discovered just how important completion is to Ryder the day we went hiking into the woods of the Big Thicket. We like the outdoors and nature. When we have a day where we don't know what to do, we might take a walk, prune the yard, or go fishing.

William was home on a slow weekend, and we had the bright idea to drive out to the Big Thicket to hike an old trail William and I frequented before kids. It was a spur of the moment trip, so we packed a light emergency bag, and threw the kids in the car. We were off! The trail we chose was a large circle which made it simple enough not to get lost, but it was a seven mile circle.

It was midday when we started this spontaneous (and idiotic) hike, in the middle of June in East Texas. Not even half way into the trail, we were already dying of heat stroke. To top it off, I was certain we were going to catch West Nile virus from the swarms of blood-sucking mosquitos attacking us. They didn't seem the least bit deterred by our bug repellant. William, the girls, and I were *done* with the family adventure by this point, and we decided to turn around and head back to civilization. Oh no, Ryder wasn't having it. He loved the hiking trail because it was a path he could follow until *completion*, and he wasn't going to turn around mid-way. We had to make a decision. Either we kept going in an attempt to finish the trail with the possibility that we would die from the heat and disease, or we turn around and carry Ryder out of the forest, kicking and screaming. We turned around.

Usually, I get a little rush of excitement while hiking through the dense forest. I find myself looking over my shoulder at every little noise and keeping a close eye on the kids, contemplating exactly how I will pry them from the jaws of anything that jumps out to eat them. Thanks to how loud Ryder was all the way back to the car, I didn't have to keep an eye out for wild animals at all. I guarantee he scared every living creature within a fifteen mile radius away. The animal population probably disappeared from that area that day, leaving mystified park rangers in their wake.

We had passed a couple of boy scouts who were exiting the trail as we were entering. Since we had turned around, they were now somewhere ahead of us. I knew they were hearing the echoing roars of Ryder's emotional pain coming, and they probably assumed an arm had been broken or someone had been snake-bit. I just knew the police, fire department, and ambulance service were going to be waiting for us at the trail head.

However, when we finally came upon our vehicle, to my surprise the emergency services were not there. Forcing Ryder into his car seat and having to practically sit on him to get him buckled up, we headed toward the closest McDonalds to get him fries to calm him down. We were tired, sweaty, stinky, itchy, irritated, and I had a terrible headache. We vowed never to make this trip with Ryder again unless it was in the winter.

Every day we come upon the Iceberg of BROKEN. Please note: If it is out of a certain order, doesn't match, won't stand up on its own, is missing a color or number, gets unintentionally wet, won't turn on, won't open, gets bumped, is cracked, or is actually split in half, it is "broken," and Ryder wants nothing else to do with it. Sometimes he even tosses the item(s) across the room.

The pressure is real. Ryder currently has *zero* patience for anything which is "broken." It does not matter if you are cooking with hot grease or using the toilet, if something becomes "broken" in this house, you had better get a move on. The Iceberg of Broken is one reason behind the constant commotion around here. Ryder freaks because something is "broken," and if the person closest to him is unable to attend to him, he or she yells for someone else in the house to hurry! Many times we have thrown our hands up in the air and told Ryder, "Yes. It's broken," because we have been unable to fix the problem. We simply have to walk away and let him throw a fit until he grows too tired to care.

Once, while we were driving home from picking up Dawn's BFF Rebecca, Ryder requested a large rectangular chocolate bar. Since Rebecca was sitting in the backseat next to Ryder, she offered to open it for him. Seems harmless enough, right?

Chapter 10—It's BROKEN!

Dawn handed Rebecca the chocolate bar, and we could hear the wrapper began to crinkle as Rebecca's fingers started a small tear in the top of the dark deliciousness. Suddenly, Dawn and I realized Rebecca did not know about BROKEN. Simultaneously, we hollered, "Don't let it break!"

Rebecca started laughing loudly at first, but she immediately ceased what she was doing and froze, candy bar dangling in her hands when she realized that Dawn and I were totally serious. Unlike Rebecca, we understood the severity of the situation and how quickly our sweet car ride could turn into a ride through hell with a Ryder who had a broken chocolate bar. That chocolate bar was the only one we had, and there wasn't a gas station for miles around. Poor Rebecca blurted out, "I am so frightened. What is going to happen if I break it?" (She opened it like a pro though.)

Because "It's broken!' is heard daily in our house and can be a bit frustrating, I've considered teaching Ryder to use other words such as "ruined" or "destroyed" in place of "broken," but would it really matter?

We often joke in our house about how perfect Ryder's wife will have to be. That woman will have to have it *all* in place and *all* together because of the Iceberg of Broken.

I imagine a future where Ryder and his wife sit down to eat dinner:

Ryder: "Why are we having corn with pork chops? Corn doesn't go with pork chops."

Wife: "Well, that's all we had for a vegetable side. I will stop by the store t…"

(Ryder cuts her off)

Ryder: "It's BROKEN!"

(Ryder tosses his dinner plate across the room)

Wife: "That's it. I'm leaving."

Now that I consider tossed corn with a side of divorce as a possible future for Ryder, I think maybe we should hang on to the hope he will outgrow "broken" or that he will find some other way to express his disappointments. Yeah, we had better stick with the therapy sessions.

11

Screw the Cake and Balloons

RYDER *LOVES* PARTIES. MAYBE HE WILL BE A PARTY PLANNER WHEN HE IS an adult. Birthday parties are his favorite events beside Christmas and Easter. Since I love to see him smile that huge grin of his and hear that squeal of happiness, I use everyone's birthday in the house and nearly every holiday for an excuse to blow up balloons and have a party. (No party poopers are allowed at our place.)

Teaching him the presents are not always for him has been tasking. That reality is difficult for most children and there is still room for improvement with Ryder, but he has made a lot of progress. He has gone from snatching presents off the table and ripping them open to gently poking the packages while giggling.

Birthday invitations for Ryder are always appreciated, but when Ryder was younger, we really had to consider the location of where the party was going to be. If it was a public place, we would usually RSVP a polite "No." There were just one or two friend's houses I felt comfortable taking Ryder to. There was one family's house I considered our most safe house to have a playdate or birthday party at. Safe as in, they had three young children too and we parented similarly so it was ok for the kids to play in or out of the house while we got to drink coffee and catch up. Safe as in their kids had known Ryder since he was born and I had never seen them treat him differently. Then, I just don't know what happened.

Their child who is closest in age to Kay was having a birthday party, and we were all invited. Just like any other party in the past I was told all the kids were welcome. Dawn chose to stay home this go-around. She had reached an age where a young child's birthday party wasn't her scene. Ryder was excited though, and so were Kay and I because any reason to eat cake and hang out with friends is reason enough. It was a pretty long drive to their house, but I knew it would work out well because, once we arrived, the kids could get out to burn off energy and have a good time.

When we got to their house, the kids played outside on the play equipment. Kay took off toward her friends as soon as the car stopped. Logan was waking up so I had a sleepy baby in my arms, and since we hadn't seen many of the guests in a while, I was surrounded by smiling people and questions as soon as Ryder, Logan, and I walked in. Well, Ryder knew where we were. Instead of joining the crowd of birthday party kids, he wanted to play in the designated toy area so he walked down the hall in that direction. I saw no problem. Ryder is a good kid and this was the usual routine at our friend's house until he grew accustomed to the large crowd.

I went to the dining room, still chatting it up with old pals. A few minutes into conversation is when I heard Ryder start to scream at the top of his lungs. This is a specific noise he makes when he's very upset about something. It is not a common noise. It comes from deep within his diaphragm. You can almost feel the pain pouring out from inside of him. This cry cut like a knife through my heart as I rushed around the corner and entered the living room where the wailing was coming from.

It still upsets me to think back on what I saw in front of me.

Ryder was in the middle of a circle made up of nearly all the kids from the birthday party, who had come inside by now. He was very upset and was crying loudly while wildly pulling at his clothes and skin. All the kids were staring at him as if he was a freak show. Some of them were laughing. The crowd of children around him was so tight I had to drop Logan to the kitchen floor and shove kids aside to get to Ryder so I could try to calm him down. He had hit his limit. I looked around, pleading with my eyes for someone to give me an explanation of what had happened as I held back Ryder's hands from

Chapter 11–Screw the Cake and Balloons

clawing himself. My hosts' oldest child delivered the insane answer, but with an attitude which seemed as if she thought Ryder's being upset and crying was entertaining!

Apparently, our hosts' youngest child, who was Ryder's age, didn't want Ryder around the toy area, but before Ryder had been kicked out of the toy area, he found the tiniest plastic box, which he had in his hand. First of all, Ryder knows when he is being excluded on purpose, and he dislikes it as much as any other kid. He is very aware and his feelings can be hurt. Second of all, Ryder likes small items, and this little plastic box he had found was really just an insignificant item (for others). The box may have come from a happy meal toy. I knew my friend's child had so many toys that I can't believe for one moment the little box was a treasure. But our hosts' youngest child had snatched the box away from Ryder, and none of the older children or adults within the proximity even attempted to convince the child to share or let Ryder play with it for maybe a little while.

Lots of parents don't believe in making their kids share their toys with other kids. I read one mother's perspective on the subject. She felt it teaches communistic behaviors where one person feels entitled to have exactly what the next person has simply because they want it. I agree. Kids should not always have to share their toys, and I never asked for Ryder to receive special treatment because of his autism. But this was different. EVERY OTHER KID at that party had been playing with the toys in the toy area. This home was known by all of us as the house where all the kids could play with all the toys. Why was my son being singled out among all the other children? Our host was standing right behind me while Ryder's episode escalated. She heard the explanation why it was happening. Why was she not correcting her child and encouraging her to share, or at least help Ryder calm down by letting him hold the box for a little while? Surely, he would forget about it once the party games began. Why? Why? WHY?!!!

If any of my children were to take a toy away from a guest and ban them from the toy area at my house, I don't care if that toy was made of gold, my kids would be in more trouble than a North Korean defector trying to run across the DMZ!

After a few minutes, Ryder still wasn't calming down. Not only was everyone still staring, but the crowd had grown larger. I had to pick Ryder up, grab

Logan along the way out the kitchen door, and exit the house. I took my kids away from the birthday party and vowed we would never bring Ryder back to that place where he was singled out, and I haven't. My hosts never apologized for their child's behavior. They sent a text message to me that evening, telling me that they felt bad we had to leave the party early, and that I should know Ryder's fits don't bother them, that he is welcome there anytime. Again, WHAT? Actions speak louder than words.

If only one of my children was really wanted at the party, they should've invited only one. It wouldn't have been the first time, and it would've saved our friendship a very harsh blow.

I don't get my feelings hurt easily, and it takes a whole lot to offend me, but that event really hurt my kid and, therefore, it pissed me off. My husband wasn't with us, and he gave me the line of "everyone gets bullied, not to shield Ryder from the world, and blah blah blah." I know that if he was there, he would've left, too. Kay understood and didn't like the way her brother was treated. We had gone to a place we believed Ryder was safe, was understood and welcomed. His being singled out was shocking and painful. I hope he doesn't remember any of it, but his memory is one of his stronger traits. If he does remember it, at least he will also remember his momma bear diving in to rescue him from the birthday party from hell.

For the love of Pete, people, teach your children to be kind to others no matter how different they are. Teach them that material items are trash when compared to friendships.

12

The Isolation is Real

Saying that I am a social person is an understatement. I can strike up a conversation with anyone at any time. I love to meet and interact with people of all ages or backgrounds and speaking in front of a crowd might shake me up for a nanosecond, but then the feeling passes, and you can't shut me up. But my love for meeting new people and hanging out with friends has taken a huge hit since autism reared its head in our house.

Autism and isolation come hand in hand. When it is just family around, there is no pressure to pretend to be other than who we are. With Ryder, that means not worrying about how his constant nudity, meltdowns, or other quirks will rub others the wrong way. As we adjusted and tended to raising an autistic, it became easier for us to put up "walls" to the outside world than it was for us to face a world full of judgement, hostility, and unacceptance. Yep, I admit it, we chose the easy way out when things became too rough.

Years before Ryder was born, we switched from public schooling to homeschooling, I was concerned how we were going to meet other children and families or "socialize," as they call it. It didn't take us long to realize there was a much bigger homeschooling community than we estimated. Once we started our homeschool co-op, we actually had to decline outings. It became a struggle to fit our book work into a five-day week because we were so busy.

There were many days when schoolwork started after 1:00 p.m. so it's a good thing homeschooling is extremely flexible.

The co-op I was running became so large so quickly, it required extra time out of my day to keep it functioning. I didn't have extra time, and there was so much to be done. I had to delegate work to other homeschooling mothers. They were fantastic! We had field trips, science fairs, a yearbook, demonstrations from visitors who taught all of the students archery and first aid, field days, holiday parties, notable historic presentations, park days, fossil and rock exhibitions, art lessons—the list of activities went on and on.

Our co-op continued for years, running right through the birth of Ryder. There were 135 students of all grade levels attending at one point. During the run of the homeschool co-op, our kids always had something to do and someone to do it with. We were a typical busy, busy, *busy* homeschooling family. When Ryder was coming up on three years of age, he hadn't officially been diagnosed yet, and life was to the point that I was barely getting through the day. I was mimicking the White Rabbit from *Alice in Wonderland* who was always scampering about saying, "I am late. I am late. For a very important date." But the words I would actually use on a daily basis were not always that sweet, and I was not only running from one thing to the next, I was doing it with three baby White Rabbits in tow, one of them being highly disagreeable.

My husband was at work, there were daily farm chores to be done, and we had no family nearby. I was trying to homeschool two children and hold regular co-op meetings with a Ryder who didn't seem to enjoy the social schedule he was born into. I realize now the days we held co-op meetings were causing Ryder's morning routine to be screwed up. Then we would pack him in the car seat to take him to unfamiliar places full of crowds, noise, different smells, and all the other things we now know can trigger a meltdown. Poor Ryder. We were frustrated because we felt he was making our lives difficult, when the entire time Ryder was frustrated because we were making his life so painful and even more confusing for him. We now know how difficult change and transitions are for Ryder, and we take extra care to prepare him beforehand.

Eventually, I couldn't drag my family or myself through the madness of running the homeschool co-op any longer. Dawn usually ended up sitting in a quiet room or in the car with Ryder during meetings anyhow because Ryder would become the center of attention during a meltdown. It's no wonder

Chapter 12—The Isolation is Real

the girls admitted to me they were tired of the hustle and bustle too when I proposed I should step down from managing the co-op. Our family needed a time out.

A great friend of mine picked up where I left off as director of the co-op, but our family didn't make it to many meetings. Eventually we stopped going all together. With Ryder public outings were simply too much for us, and there was no one who could watch him at home while we were out. The social-whirling homeschool world we had been a big part of went on without us.

Since we didn't make it to nearly any meetings any longer, our friends would make the drive to visit us when they could, but our home was so volatile and chaotic. I am not surprised these visits became fewer and fewer. It's understandable that our friends had to continue with their own busy lives.

Our friends were not the only ones we found ourselves isolated from. My family is spread out across the states, and family members heard less and less from us. I stopped calling or connecting with family on social media and we could not dare travel to visit them. (Talk about a road trip or flight from hell.) When they would call to check in on us, conversations were usually short and polite since I was literally having to lock myself in a *bathroom* or sit outside in order for them to be able to hear me over the background commotion. The few times I reached out for advice or gave a family member some indication that we were being steamrolled by life, their words would upset me. No one in the family was familiar with autism or what it actually felt like to live in our autistic home. There were a lot of assumptions on what exactly was going on, and a lot of opinions on how we weren't doing enough correctly. It was easier to back away than continue to get upset.

Last year I realized how unhealthy our isolation had become. One of the routine procedures for the healthcare company we use for Ryder is to make an annual in-home visit. It was the first year we had used the company, and when someone contacted me by phone to set up a time and date for the in-home visit, the alarms in my head began to sound. What was the goal of this in-home visit? Will my home be inspected? Is the person who is coming over familiar with autism? Can I opt out of this visit?

The visit turned out not to be as big a deal as I had feared. We had polished our home and toilets for nothing. The nurse who came out to meet Ryder and ask questions had come to help. If Ryder had needed a wheelchair and we didn't have a ramp to the house, she would've reported back to the insurance company that our special needs kiddo needed something to help make everyday life easier. Because of our isolation, a simple act of kindness had looked suspicious.

As the healthcare representative was leaving, I walked her to her car and voiced my silly concerns I had had before her visit. She assured me our home was not controversial in any way, and she had seen much worse. Without breaking any confidentiality agreements, she briefly described an in-home visit where she pulled into the driveway only to find the mother of an autistic child frantic because her son had climbed up onto the roof and she couldn't get him to come down. I sighed with relief. That had not happened here *yet*.

Yes, every autistic family is different, and some struggle much more than others when it comes to socializing with friends and family.

On a rare visit last year, I was sitting with a friend at our dining room table, and we were chatting over a cup of coffee. She was telling me about a mother who had started attending her church. The mother was our age and she kept to herself. She had two sons who came to church with her, a two-year-old and a six-year-old. The oldest son who was six was autistic and completely non-verbal. He had an iPad he brought to church, but from what she gathered, he wasn't using it to communicate with yet. His iPad was used more for entertainment purposes. The mother of the autistic son was reaching out to my friend a little at a time. Over this short time span, my friend had learned that this mother put up with quite a bit of verbal abuse from her husband, who had hardly anything to do with his autistic child, yet held a great relationship with the typical two-year-old. The boys were brothers from the same parents, but the father chose to pick favorites between his two sons. Maybe he is one of the dads who doesn't know how to interact with his autistic son, but if he is verbally abusive to his wife, my bet is on his being more of a finger-pointer who expects perfection and is likely to shun those who seem less than perfect.

Regardless, I told my friend the treatment of the six-year-old made me sick to my stomach. The young autistic boy still had feelings, and I strongly believed he could tell the difference in how his dad treated him compared to his younger brother, which must have hurt his heart. I also brought it to her attention how the boy's mother must be suffering from isolation.

"You should schedule a playdate with her and the boys or invite her over," I suggested. "She must feel so alone in her situation. If her son is autistic, he may not do too well outside the familiarity of his home and church. She sounds like she needs a good friend."

"That's exactly what I am going to do," my friend agreed. "You are right; I hadn't considered how she must not be able to get out often, to take her mind off of things or to make friends."

I used to live with the same mindset as my friend. I was not intentionally being rude, but I was unaware of what families of special needs children live through daily and how much a struggle their daily life can be. I don't know how that all played out with my friend and the mother, but I hope things are better for them since last year.

I am tired of isolation.

I know the girls are too, so I am really looking forward to Ryder and Kay joining the swim team next month. I finally have the guts to try to get back into a healthy social groove. When I contacted the team's representative to get a feel for how we may or may not fit in and to request the age requirements, I was told one of the head coaches has an autistic child. So at least someone there knows where we are coming from. Rumor has it, the local swim team is packed full of homeschoolers too, so we will keep our fingers crossed.

13

We Have Our Reasons

I AM USED TO STRANGE LOOKS OR QUESTIONS WHEN PEOPLE ARE TOLD WE homeschool our children. Homeschooling is becoming a huge movement across the country, but public schools still dominate the education system—dare I assume even more so when it comes to special needs kids? Homeschooling "neurotypical" children already requires you to boldly go where most parents have never gone, and I haven't run into many parents who have homeschooled their autistic child. It is doubly a challenge, pressured by your own doubts that you can provide your autistic child with what he/she really needs.

When Ryder began receiving therapy, I was asked to write a letter for their records stating that we were aware free speech and occupational therapies were available to Ryder in the public school system, but that we were opting out of the public school resources available to him. Oh, and of course they wanted reasons *why* we had made this decision.

I had to laugh internally at this request. Though I didn't have to bring the letter home to write it. Without hesitation, I asked the therapist for a pen and paper. I knew this moment had been coming, simply because I had struggled within myself about what would be best for Ryder, so I knew others would eventually question our decision too. I had ready my mental list of reasons. I composed the letter, signed it, and handed the clipboard back to the therapist with a smile.

We had already been homeschooling our oldest daughters for close to four years before Ryder came into our world. Homeschooling works better for our family because of William's work schedule (and the fact that we all love to sleep in), but for many other reasons, too. Ironically though, Ryder's initial diagnosis was actually accomplished through the public school system because a friend who knew of my growing concern told me I could get him tested for free at our local public school instead of paying a psychologist hundreds of dollars out of pocket.

I made an appointment, and off we went on our field trip to see what our tax dollars were paying for, and for my kids to see what a public school looked like on the inside.

About a week after we answered a million questions by filling in those small bubbles with a number two pencil, and the making of one video of how Ryder "played" while he was being followed around by four therapists studying him as if he were a strange undiscovered species, we were told they had come to a decision, and wanted to meet with us.

We left Ryder with Dawn on the morning of the meeting since it was only expected to take an hour. When my husband Logan and I arrived for the ARD (Admission, Review, and Dismissal) meeting, we were directed to the special education wing of the school and asked to wait in the hallway as the meeting room was currently being used. Our escort left to go back to her station. There was a teacher in the same hallway as us, putting together the sweetest bulletin board of an oversized flower garden. I watched her while we waited and remember being very impressed with what she was able to create with the brightly colored tissue paper.

From where we were we couldn't see in to the special education classroom, but we were able to hear everything. Somewhere in that room, amongst the stimming noises and banging of toys, we heard a little boy who was getting frustrated. He began to cry louder and louder saying "I want my brother" over and over again. Even though Ryder didn't talk much yet, I immediately noticed the similarities in the way this little boy's frustration was escalating and how Ryder's frustration could escalate. I had been reading everything I could get my hands on about autism by this time, and I knew that the child

Chapter 13 – We Have Our Reasons

we heard needed some calming techniques from his teachers, and fast, or else this episode was going to hit the fan.

Instead of calming techniques, we heard a teacher raise her voice at the boy. She told him to go to some area of the room (maybe a corner). When the banshee teacher finally got him there, she continued to lash out at him, "You had better quiet down!"

WHAT?!! I couldn't take it. I was on the verge of running in there in an attempt to help this little boy and possibly punching the banshee in the face. Tears of anger were forming in my eyes as the tongue lashing went on and on. This teacher's treatment of the poor child was insane and inexcusable.

My husband doesn't mess around when it comes to the safety of our children. By this point, he had picked Logan up and was heading out the front doors of the building. We have been married for a long time, and I knew he was thinking something like, "Hell, no. My kid will not be treated like that."

The tissue paper artist in the hallway had been nervously glancing at us. When my husband went to leave, she dropped her supplies and hurried around the corner to the classroom. The banshee teacher stopped screaming, and I think she was told to leave the classroom. Right then, the doors to the meeting room opened and five smiling faces were staring at us, welcoming and urging us to join them for the ARD meeting. We hesitantly entered the meeting room and sat down as they went over the test, their findings, and recommendations for our three-year-old almost completely non-verbal son.

They told us he was definitely somewhere on the "spectrum," and they wanted to bring another psychologist from the closest major city to administer a final test, but they highly recommended Ryder immediately begin their special education program, as in the very next day. This proposed schedule of theirs would put Ryder in the same vicinity as the screaming banshee teacher 8:00 a.m. to 4:00 p.m., Monday through Friday.

My husband didn't say anything. I think he was still trying to calm down from what we had heard going on earlier. I had only one question for them, yet I had to ask it twice to get an answer.

I asked, "What kind of calming techniques do your teachers use because Ryder is known to get frustrated and have meltdowns?" I was told that meltdowns are not uncommon, and sometimes they even have to give the parent a call to get some suggestions. Apparently, one child had had a meltdown recently, and they had called the mother. The mother told them to simply take off his socks. Problem solved. (Mother knows better than strangers.)

Okay, but that was not an answer to my question. So I asked again, "Yes, but what kind of steps are in place to calm down a frustrated child, like the upset child we heard in the other room before we came in here?" None of these smiling ladies had an answer for me. A dead silence hung in the air for at least ten seconds. Then the principal of the school who was sitting directly across from me at the long table leaned forward, made her Cheshire cat smile even bigger, and said, "We treat them like one of our own."

REALLY? That was the only answer I could get?? No thank you. Goodbye. We will contact you with our final decision.

We sent a letter:

*Dear T*****,*

We greatly appreciate all the help you provided to us through the evaluation of our son, Ryder, and the information you provided to us during the recent ARD meeting. We had our suspicions that Ryder's brain worked differently than most other children's brains do, and, thanks to you and your team, we were able to receive the confirmation we needed.

At this time, we do not feel it is necessary for Ryder to be evaluated again. A second evaluation seems redundant to us, considering we've received the answers we needed through your program.

We currently have the time, money, space, and resources available to us for Ryder to receive daily speech therapy lessons as well as daily lessons in everyday life tasks or experiences in his home setting.

We also strongly feel the home is the best place for him to learn right now considering his age and the fact that he is comfortable with his routines and environment here. His nutrition is something we will be able to monitor easier at home too.

Once again, we would like to express our thanks to you and your team for taking the time to listen to our concerns and provide a confirmation for us that the issues we see in Ryder are valid.

With sincere thanks,

William & Jennifer Hayword.

Chapter 13 —We Have Our Reasons

Looking back, I regret not adding some harsh language, but I have no regrets about our decision. I believe it was one of the best decisions we made concerning Ryder's autism because two years after this charade, Ryder has mastered and continues to master all of his academic, speech, and occupational therapy goals.

We all know that the public schools in the United States get money for each student who attends daily. (Which explains the insane truancy arrests parents are facing around the country.) I found out later that the public school system can receive *more than double the money* for each special needs student who attends daily. If this is what is driving the push to enroll special needs three-year-olds into a system where the staff is overwhelmed or not properly trained, lessoning the quality and effectiveness of the program to the point that the child is suffering, it is sickening and shameful.

As a matter of fact, the Texas public school system has recently found itself in trouble for failing to provide special needs children with the services and attention they require to do well in school. Many public school districts plan to throw billions of dollars at the problem. What is the money going to pay for? It is supposed to pay the salaries of more therapists and teachers of special needs children, but there is a problem with this expensive solution. There simply are not *enough* therapists and teachers trained and available to lower the special needs student-to-teacher ratio. The number of special needs children in public school is rising so quickly, the system cannot keep up.

My advice to any parent who has a special needs student and cannot homeschool or does not wish to homeschool is to push yourself even further than you have before to advocate for your child. Be the parent who shows up at all the school board meetings, participates in all school activities, and raises money for video cameras to be installed in special needs classrooms. Substitute as often as possible and educate everyone around you. Really make your and your child's voice be heard.

Be the change that needs to take place for the future of your child and for other children like yours who will follow. Because there will be more children to come and there are bound to be more banshee teachers as well.

Not everyone has the option of homeschooling their children, and my heart goes out to those individuals who are up against a government-run system that is not always able to meet the needs of the children. As for us, homeschooling is currently what we are able to provide, and it is the best option for Ryder and for our family. So I say, "God Bless America, the land where we still have the freedom to raise our children the way we see fit, to advocate for those who cannot speak-out for themselves, and to stand up against those who want to take that right away from parents."

14

How About Those Doctors?

OUR CHILDREN WERE ALL PERFECT EXAMPLES OF PHYSICAL HEALTH WHEN they were born. Every one of them was at *least* a whopping eight pounds at birth, and I breastfed all of them with ease.

I used a pediatrician's services on a regular basis with Dawn because she was my firstborn and I was inexperienced. I also rushed Dawn to the emergency room every time her fever went above 102 degrees, she had any sign of congestion, for any rash, cut, and for any other minor incident. Finally, I realized that all these visits were doing was costing us money and causing us stress. They would send us home with a triple dose of ibuprofen after hours of numerous pokes or tests, and then a huge bill would arrive in the mail. So pediatrician visits turned into extremely rare things with Kay, Ryder, and Logan. Only an absolute emergency would have me hauling our children into the germy fray of a pediatrician's office, and we never really had any emergencies.

This may come as a surprise to some people, but many kids don't have to be rushed to the doctor to receive antibiotics for every little sickness they contract. Lots of times their immune systems have the ability to fight back for them. No joke.

When Ryder came into our world, we were still vaccinating our children though. Ryder had vaccines up to four months of age before we stopped torturing him and the family. We did not stop administering vaccines to Ryder because we were worried about the side effects of the vaccines. We initially called it quits with his vaccines for other, louder, and more nerve-wracking reasons. Ryder was straight-screaming on the ride to the clinic, straight-screaming while we were there, straight-screaming as the vaccines were being administered, and of course straight-screaming at home for *days*. For what? We homeschool our children! We decided, "Screw these trips to get vaccines just because everyone else was getting them." The visits to the clinic stopped. There was never any sickness we couldn't handle at home with over-the-counter medication nor any broken bones (a miracle in itself). We went on with our lives.

When Logan was born, we were teetering on the edge of considering Ryder possibly autistic, so naturally we discovered the claims that vaccines caused autism. For this reason, we opted out of vaccinating Logan completely. (Fast forward to almost three years later, we now strongly believe vaccines did *not* cause Ryder's autism, and we have considered getting the boys caught up on their shots. But I do ponder over the strange reasoning behind the massive amount of suspicious biologic serums that are recommended to be pumped into children before the age of one. It's a bit alarming for massive amounts of *any* foreign substance to be injected into tiny babies, isn't it? Isn't it?)

Anyhow…could Ryder's autism have been spotted earlier if he had seen a pediatrician more often? Possibly, but we wouldn't have been able to get him into therapy sooner. We would still have had to do the research and start home therapy on our own because we lived in such a rural area, the out-of-pocket cost for therapy was through the roof, and there was no way he was going to spend time with a banshee teacher.

Shortly after Ryder's first diagnosis and our move back to the town we had lived in when Dawn was a baby, we decided Ryder needed regular pediatrician visits to get him accustomed to the poking, prodding, the smells, and everything else a doctor's visit included. After all, the chain of paperwork to receive therapy begins with a prescription and requires constant evaluation to track progress or regression. Visits to the doctor will be a regular part of Ryder's life.

The pediatrician I had used when Dawn was younger was still practicing. He was someone I had respected, and I wouldn't have hesitated to recommend

Chapter 14—How About Those Doctors?

his services to a total stranger. Naturally, I decided to use his services again for Ryder and Logan.

At his initial appointment, Ryder did great getting height and weight measurements with the nurse before Doc Dodo came in the room. Doc Dodo did ask me for the reason of the visit, but he hardly let me answer before he dove into a lengthy lecture on the importance of Ryder being vaccinated. You would've thought he was a drill sergeant from a 1960s boot camp and I hadn't shined my shoes properly by the way he was intensely scolding me. We were only at his office to get Ryder used to regular check-ups, but instead I received a disrespecting mouthful from Doc Dodo not only on our lack of vaccines, but he also scolded me with:

"You are not a speech therapist."

"You are not a teacher."

"Ryder needs to be put into public school."

Who in the Hell-O did he think he was? It had been eleven years since he was Dawn's pediatrician and my experience as a parent of four children had given me a heck of a lot more useful knowledge than his medical degree when it came to the well-being of *my* children. I had no concern with my boys not being fully vaccinated, Logan is the healthiest of all our children and he hasn't had a single injection his entire life! I knew the decision to homeschool *our* children was proving to be the best decision for our family—the results spoke for themselves. I had already begun pre-school with Ryder, and we were registering with a local speech and occupational facility outside the home. I wasn't trying to do *everything* on my own.

I was beyond pissed and frustrated as I paid for our lecture and then stormed out of Doc. Dodo's office. We asked Ryder's speech therapist if she knew of any other Doc in town (preferably one who was familiar with autism) and we made an appointment with Doctor B.

Doc B was an exceptional example of what a Doc should be. I was so touched by the care we received at her office that I wrote the entire staff a thank you letter once we were home. Doc B took the time to meet Ryder, interact with him, and to listen to our story. It was such a calm and smooth visit that Ryder didn't seem to notice the poking, prodding, and strange smells. The doctor found nothing wrong with the style of parenting we had chosen and assured me that if we bumped into any other health care "professionals" who had a problem with our decision to stop vaccinating, I could give them her phone number and she would handle them. Through her referral to Texas Children's Hospital Neurology Department, we were able to get the proper diagnosis for Ryder to continue regular speech and occupational therapy outside the home.

Upon our visit to the Neurology Department of Texas Children's, I immediately knew they were familiar with autism. Their offices were on an upper floor so as soon as we exited the elevator, I began visually mapping out the office to locate any possible exits from the waiting room Ryder would use to bolt from while I was checking in. There were none. There were also no railings he could climb or flip over. It was a fully enclosed, comfortable waiting room, painted a darker shade of blue, and the lights were dim, unlike the blaring florescent lights at most places. The TV was low in volume and the toys were very engaging, full of patterns, colors, and gears. The staff was patient with Ryder and understanding about his occasional lack of compliance. We had a very pleasant experience there.

We did have to meet with a CPS worker before we left. I understood it was routine procedure, but I was still a little nervous and on the defensive side, especially after our previous visit with Doc Dodo. As a mother of an autistic child and a homeschool mother, I know there are some things about our unconventional way of living which might be judged or frowned upon by others. I smiled politely the entire time and gave her a chance. She had good questions and concerns regarding our homeschooling set up and Ryder's home life. CPS workers get a bum rap, but I know that CPS worker we met with meant well. She was doing her job the same way I do my best at mothering.

When it comes to raising children, doctors are important, teachers are important, therapists are important, but a parent's insight is *critical*. Parents know how to communicate with their children better than anyone else. We can tell when something is terribly off and needs medical attention or how to teach them something they may be struggling to understand. We know what our children need and do not need to get through the day. The world would do well to remember that we know who our children are *beyond* statistics, rules, or definitions.

15

To Medicate or Not to Medicate

A FRIEND ASKED ME HOW I BELIEVE OUR COUNTRY WILL HANDLE THE impending steep rise in autism. Her mother is a school teacher and told my friend how difficult balancing the classroom can be with only two of her twenty-five students being autistic. Without hesitation, I answered her, "They will do it with drugs."

Somewhere in this book I jokingly stated that I wanted more of whatever it was they injected Ryder with at a dental visit. In all honesty, I wouldn't feel comfortable medicating my child other than in a situation similar to the dental visit because we have learned to get through the day without medication. That's us. Not everyone is able to manage their autistic child's fits or self-abusive behavior. I am not judging.

It's just that "Kids on drugs" has taken on an entirely different meaning since I was in school. Our slogan used to be *D.A.R.E. to Say No to Drugs* and we would have school rallies or parades where we would receive red ribbons emphasizing the importance of not trying gateway drugs which could lead to being a crack addict. These days, kids are still using the common illegal drugs from my school years, but now they are also able to legally take drugs given to them by adults.

I repeat, it is now acceptable in our society for certain adults to give drugs to little kids. Kids are popping pills left and right. The doctors are the drug dealers. They label it "medication" and get everyone to believe the drug is necessary in order for the kid to be normal in school or in social situations. Normal is overrated. Maybe in some situations the drugs can help take the edge off of the kid's extreme behavior, but I know from experience that doctors are usually too quick to prescribe drugs to young kids.

It's especially common for autistic children who are Ryder's age to be on drugs, even before other safer methods to get through the day are attempted. We had to switch pediatricians yet again once Ryder was approved for state disability medical coverage, and regulation required he be seen by the new doc to continue therapy. We were late to the initial doctor's appointment, and I stupidly drove past McDonald's without stopping. At that point our morning became a lot more complicated. Ryder was mad and he stayed mad for the entire length of the appointment. We couldn't skip out on this appointment because we needed a referral for Ryder's occupational therapy, so I dug in my heels, and didn't make eye contact with any other person in the doctor's office as I held Ryder while he raged on like a wild hog with his foot caught in a snare. On the plus side, we were called back to a room quicker than usual. (I imagine the office staff were tired of hearing Ryder and they were worried he would break something.) The *first* thing our new Doc said to me when he walked through the office door was, "I can prescribe one of two medications for him."

I declined and told Doc that Ryder wasn't always as bad as he was being at the moment, but that he hadn't gotten something he wanted and we needed to wait out his tantrum. See how quickly Doc wanted to give my kid drugs, though? He's a decent doctor, but his automatic response to a child who is not acting "normally" is to drug them.

Our son doesn't need to be drugged. He needs to be taught how to adapt to the world around him. And the world around him needs to be taught that being different is okay.

He needs patience, acceptance, and discipline just like any other child. Getting him off of his French fries addiction wouldn't hurt either. I am sure, as his diet improves, so will his attitude. (It is all a work in progress.)

The rush to drug the children is exactly why early intervention is so important, and I wish for an unobtainable utopian world where early intervention programs *always* include the family.

Chapter 15–To Medicate or Not to Medicate

If we did decide to drug Ryder, I know it would be a selfish act on our part. I will not deny that the thought *has* crossed my mind before because Ryder can really push my buttons, but how would it help *him*? What are the long-term effects of these drugs on kids? Does anyone *really* know? Or will we see commercials in fifteen years urging autistic adults who were prescribed XYZ as children and are now suffering from horrible side effects to contact a lawyer for a settlement?

We've all heard about the anger that outsourcing has stirred up in the United States for the past decade, right? I am mad about outsourcing for more than financial reasons. There are currently medications being recalled by the FDA because these medications contain poisons. How do these poisons get into our medications? The country the U.S. outsourced manufacturing jobs to does *not* regulate medicinal ingredients like our government does. And the icing on this carcinogenic cake is that more than half of the medications being distributed around the globe have ingredients made in these unregulated factories! *More than half, y'all!* That means the medications these drug dealers are prescribing for children have a very real chance of containing crap that will do them more harm than good.

Let me reiterate, I am not judging. But I am angry. How many times have I been in the waiting room of Ryder's therapy office, met a new patient and the family then a few weeks go by after their initial autism diagnosis. The next time I see the kiddo he or she is *zombified* because the kiddo has been drugged by a doctor and now the poor child has a round of side effects which range from extremely aggressive behavior to insomnia. The crazy part is that most of these side effects are simply treated by *more* drugs! It's madness!

Giving kiddos drugs to make them pay attention in school doesn't seem logical to me either. Sure Ryder can't sit still for too long while we do bookwork, but he is five. If anything seems normal to me, it is the idea that a five-year-old won't sit still for hours on end. That has nothing to do with his being autistic. If I am trying to teach Ryder something new and he isn't quite getting it, we take a different approach. We have gone outside to do schoolwork, written our ABCs in the sand with sticks, learned songs to get the subject across, or simply taken a break from school for the day to visit the zoo.

If he won't learn the way I am teaching, I will teach the way he learns.

As for depression or anxiety pills for children, I am also very wary. Has the child received enough sunshine for the day? How about exercise? Isn't it a scientifically proven fact that both of these things make your brain create endorphins? Maybe the child needs a puppy, some chores to feel accomplished and better about himself, or simply some time alone with mom or dad.

Yes, the times they are a changing! "Give em some drugs." seems to be the solution for nearly every child who doesn't' naturally conform to society's box of normality. There are drug doctors pushing pills on kids and then there are the natural remedy folk pushing cannabis and changing laws across the country.

CBD oil is one thing, but teaching a minor how to *smoke* weed!? What are we thinking? I've seen the social media posts. I know the THC can decrease self-harming behavior, can even stop seizures or do other amazing things without the poisonous side effect of pills. But *smoking* it takes it to a whole new level.

I close my eyes and imagine my little man Ryder having a meltdown so I light up and pass him a joint of some highly concentrated genetically modified sticky hash for him to inhale into his little lungs—simply so I don't have to restrain him or hear him scream. And I cringe.

What a great habit to teach our future generations. Puff Puff Pass.

What an uninvolved and detached way to parent a child who has great potential.

I am not a doctor, but I am a mother, and when it comes to my kids I would suggest they try a lifestyle change before popping or smoking drugs. This new wave of drugging the young children in our country gives an entirely new meaning to the phrase, "Using gateway drugs."

Since I am already an adult and my bad habits are established, I have joked about starting a club for autistic parents where we can meet weekly to sit around and medicate ourselves with CBD oil, wine, and chocolate, followed by espresso shots, before we need to jump back into the daily grind of raising autism. (Hey, I can dream.)

But let me be crystal clear: I wouldn't feel comfortable drugging Ryder since he is so young and still developing. Period.

16

I am Mother, and I am Guilty of Giving Into Manipulative Behavior

RYDER HAS BEEN RECEIVING SPEECH THERAPY FOR OVER A YEAR NOW, AND he was just approved for occupational therapy last month. Ryder's autism comes with sensory issues and occupational therapy is supposed to help him get his sensory issues to a level where he can eventually function independently in society. Obviously, a new type of therapy means a new therapist, and a new therapist means a new person who must learn Ryder's quirks and squeaks in order to make any progress with him.

So this new therapist called me into the hallway of the therapy office last week to talk about Ryder. Ryder had been pretty pissed off for a little over an hour that session because he wasn't in agreement with what was being asked of him. He wanted to call the shots and was refusing to jump on the trampoline. Ryder *loves* the trampoline. He was simply testing the waters with the new therapist. I, two other mothers, and the rest of the office had the pleasure of hearing his vocal protest reverberate off the walls for that hour while I sat there waiting for the inevitable pediatric evaluation of the situation.

Then I was asked to come into the hallway with the therapist.

Here was this young woman, who was just getting to know Ryder, telling me in a very serious tone, that my son's current meltdown wasn't a sensory meltdown. She stated he was having a behavioral meltdown. As my right eye began to twitch uncontrollably, the therapist went on to tell me that my son has *learned* manipulative behavior over the course of his lifetime, and that I needed to know how to spot the difference between manipulative behavior and a sensory meltdown, and *never* give into the manipulative behavior in order to help Ryder.

Let's see, (eye roll) Ryder's manipulative behaviors summed up: Screaming a scream that could break glass, whining, melting limply to the ground, biting himself, scratching himself, hitting himself, throwing things, or going stiff as a board. (Note that each one of these acts comes with an insane amount of unshakable sustainability). Yes, I am aware these are happening when they happen.

I politely smiled, thanked her, and ensured her that we will try to work on that area.

Inside my mind I was thinking, "Hello?? It's so easy to stand there telling me not to give in, but, sister, you just don't know! When I am struggling to get four kids out the door and Ryder decides he doesn't want to wear shoes so he starts to melt to the ground while fake-crying or wants to throw his shoes across the room, I could seriously care less about not giving into his manipulative behavior. The kid can go barefoot to the car. I don't care. If you had been living inside our hazardous minefield for the past five years, you wouldn't care either."

Now don't get me wrong. We love and respect Ryder's therapists. We may have figured out quite a bit on our own, but these therapists have given us some gold medal tips and strategies. The method which has changed our lives the most is the Fun Chart. I will take credit for the title, but the idea of the chart started at therapy sessions. Ryder is drawn to numbers or things in order. He wants to know what is coming next in his day and he thrives on routine. He was creating his own routine for years based on what he wanted to do, but as he gets older he needs to get certain things accomplished in his day, such as attempting to dress himself or practicing his writing, and he isn't always an eager beaver to follow orders. The Fun Chart makes Ryder so much more accepting of the daily tasks he needs to complete.

Chapter 16—I am Mother, and I am Guilty of Giving Into Manipulative Behavior

The chart is a piece of paper with sixteen boxes or less on it. The boxes are numbered, and contain simple, hand-drawn pictures of what he needs to accomplish in order. Each day is usually the same, but with a few twists, so I take a moment each evening or morning to sketch out stick drawings onto a new chart. The charts help keep him focused, to learn, and to feel accomplished. One of the best things about them is they are meant to be disposable. Ryder really loves crossing off each task as he completes it. I am all for killing two birds with one stone, and the charts teach him sequencing, counting, and they offer practice for how to properly hold a pencil when he crosses off a box he has completed. Add these to the fact his chart is already full of tasks which help him, and I call that killing a flock of birds with one stone!

Tomorrow Ryder has therapy so his chart looks like this: #1 Brush hands and feet with sensory brush. #2 Brush teeth. #3: Get dressed. #4 Eat breakfast. #5 Mom's car. #6 Therapy with your favorite therapist. #7 Pick up Pizza. #8 Go Home

A typical school day looks like this: #1 Brush hands and feet with sensory brush. #2 Brush teeth. #3 Get dressed. #4 Eat breakfast. #5 Swing. (Vestibular activity) #6 Trampoline. (Proprioceptive activity) #7: PlayDoh animals. (Tactile activity) #8 Eat Lunch. #9 Tracing shapes. #10 Storytime. #11 Number Puzzle. #12 Velcro learning she/he. #13 TV/Rest time. #14 Outside Play #15 Dinnertime. #16 Bath, Brush, Bed.

This is something new for us, and it doesn't always go as smooth as 1-2-3. Ryder really didn't want to trace shapes holding a pencil the other day, and we spent so much time throwing a fit, taking a break, throwing a fit, then taking a break, then eventually tracing with our fingers that we never finished the chart that was planned, but we did eventually get the shapes traced. It was good enough for me.

I think these charts will be a big part of how Ryder transitions into independent adulthood. Eventually, we can add a set time to each activity instead of the activities being numbered. As of now, I have integrated the charts into other areas of our household since they are an easy way to give the other kids their daily chore lists.

I don't think Ryder's sisters call their charts full of chores "fun charts" though.

17

Literally, Dude

When Ryder's speech therapist came to ask me if there was anything I would like Ryder to master, I told her that Ryder didn't respond if someone asked him his own name. He also didn't know my husband and me as anything other than "Mom" and "Dad." If he were to be separated from us or lost, these were basic things he would need to know. So she started working with him during their sessions, and we worked with him at home.

It wasn't too long before we were able to ask him, "What is your name?' and he would reply, "Ryder." We could ask him, "What is your daddy's name?" and he would reply, "William." It was the same thing when we asked him, "What is your mommy's name?" He would say, "Jennifer." He had it mastered.

The weather has been freezing cold one day and then sweltering hot the next (typical Texas weather). I asked Ryder on the way to the car the other day, "Are you cold?" He answered, "No, I'm Ryder." You've got to love that literal response from any child, but it meant the world to me because he answered me with three words, in a complete sentence, without hesitation, and his answer was absolutely correct. If the adult Ryder were to give that answer to a stranger though (with his Yoda style of speaking), his autism would stick out like a sore thumb.

Ryder can be silly, but he is naturally quite literal. We took Ryder trick-or-treating this past Halloween. It was only the second time he has gone, and this year he could say, "Trick-in-Treat!" Kay was a classic witch with a fantastic green face, Logan was a buff Spider-Man, and Ryder made a great pirate. He even wore the pirate captain hat. We loaded Kay, Ryder, Logan, and our little red wagon into the SUV, and we hauled them to the closest neighborhood. With everyone dressed up differently and acting goofy for one night out of the year, Ryder fit right in. He would run up to the door with Kay, holler, "Trick-in-treat!" and eagerly await the surprise they would slip into his treat bag, then run back down the driveway to search his bag for the newest addition of candy to decide if he wanted to eat it immediately, save it for later, or toss it into Logan's bag if it was candy he disliked.

During the longer lulls while we walked around the blocks, Ryder would jump into the wagon with Logan to take a break and observe all the costumes passing him. He would yell out any costume he recognized, "Spider-man!" "Scooby-Doo!" "Spooky Ghost!" and then he pointed toward something, but hesitated to speak. It had been raining off and on that Halloween Day, and it was starting to drizzle a little. Ryder was pointing at an adult carrying an open umbrella. He hesitated, figuring out this person's costume. Then he yelled, "Isa, Isa Umbrella!" the same way a gold miner would yell, "Eureka!" Again, he was correct in my eyes, but his autism was apparent to strangers around us.

William met a new co-worker today who has a six-year-old autistic daughter. He told me how this gentleman's daughter had improved socially to the point that her autism is nearly invisible to the untrained eye because she has been attending ABA therapy. William and I have discussed ABA therapy, but because it is pretty controversial and *really* expensive, we haven't jumped on the bandwagon yet. I don't think there is an ABA therapy facility within seventy-five miles of us anyhow.

When I first heard of ABA therapy, I found a few articles written by adult autistics and they all said ABA therapy robbed them of their childhood because of how hardcore it is. ABA therapists suggest thirty to forty hours of therapy a week for a three-year-old! The kid may as well be working a full time job! ABA therapy, from their perspective, reminded me of dog training where they were rewarded for good or "normal" behavior, but scolded or not rewarded for autistic behaviors. That was enough to sway my decision at the moment.

Chapter 17—Literally, Dude

I am all for kids getting to enjoy their childhood and totally against anything that causes a child enough grief that it follows them into their adulthood.

Then William meets a man like his co-worker, and his co-worker is not only praising the results of the therapy, but also saying that his daughter cannot wait to get to therapy each day. Suddenly, my mind starts over-working. Would it be better for Ryder to get ABA therapy? If so, when? How will we afford it? We love and enjoy Ryder the way he is. Will who he is be suppressed and hidden from us with ABA therapy? I just don't know yet. The idea is sitting on the "everything is worth a try" platter at the moment.

When Ryder was a little baby, we found that he would respond very well to music, and we used song to communicate ideas to Ryder before any diagnosis or therapist was in the picture. We made up all kinds of songs to get him to understand steps and follow through without a fight. We had a song for buckling up in the car seat, a song for brushing his teeth (that one took a while to work though), and a song for washing in the bathtub, a song for eating fruits and vegetables, and a bunch of other songs I can't remember. The Fed-Ex delivery driver caught us one-too-many times singing about washing stinky feet and armpits. When Ryder was diagnosed, I discovered there was a popular type of therapy called music therapy. I told the girls we had done well. By simply listening to our intuition we had actually been engaging in a legit therapy with Ryder!

My point is, we naturally knew what to do to get Ryder to do more than pull, push, yell, or grunt, before he could speak. I am a strong believer that parents and siblings have a powerful intuition on how to help a loved one with the setbacks autism can cause. There is no doubt that doctors and therapists can introduce a lot of new strategies, too. God knows they have helped us tremendously, but with each autistic child being different than the next, the people who are closest to the autistic child ultimately know what is best for the child. And it is not impossible for an autistic child to progress into independent adulthood without a therapy that could possibly scar him or her.

The first time I admitted out loud that I *hated* autism, Dawn told me that she likes the way Ryder's brain works because it makes him who he is and that if he wasn't autistic, he would be a different Ryder. Leave it to a teenager to put me in my place, but I think Dawn's point of view mirrors my biggest concern with ABA therapy. I don't want my son to be forced to become someone he isn't or to feel ashamed of quirks which he cannot control.

In Temple Grandin's book *The Autistic Brain*, she interviews an autistic man who says he often feels as if he is experiencing an out-of-body experience because he is able to see his body parts stimming, yet he cannot make the motion stop. Many of Ryder's quirks are automatic reactions to stimuli, not motions he necessarily makes on purpose. I would feel terrible if we trained him to believe the things which make him special to us make him a freak to the rest of the world. But is that how he will be treated by the world anyhow if he doesn't learn to hide his quirks and habits? Man, this is going to require a lot of pondering before we come to a conclusion on the topic of ABA Therapy.

18

If They Only Had a Brain...
Or Some Manners

AFTER BEING EXPOSED TO FIVE YEARS OF AUTISM, WE ARE FLEXIBLE PEOple. You know how the entire family goes to watch the piano recital? Not us. (We have learned to dodge that headache.) One parent goes and video tapes the recital for the rest of the family. Same thing goes for martial arts class, 4-H meetings, or clothes shopping. Yard sale and thrift store shopping has become a thing of the past. Ryder wants a destination and a return. Yard sales and thrift stores are too "all over the place" for him.

Some of my happiest memories as a child were the weekly trips to the public library with my grandma. The girls and I would visit the library as often as we could because I wanted them to have those great memories, too. We even kept up the library tradition for a little while after Ryder was born, until the day the librarian referred to us as "the family with the screaming child." We order our books online now, and the kids get to have the library experience *at home*. Our book collection is massive for this reason. My sweet nephew helped us move last year, and as he hauled yet another heavy box of books out of the moving van, he told me that we have an unhealthy love of books. He meant it as a compliment of course, being a person who loves to read himself.

Sometimes holidays are too much for Ryder, and we have to work around family time. This past Thanksgiving something upset Ryder, and I had to get Ryder back to our house to calm him down. For whatever reason, he didn't want to go back to Mimi and Papa's to celebrate Thanksgiving. I think he probably figured it was an oversized BBQ, not a celebration. If we had put up balloons and streamers, he may have agreed to come back to Mimi and Papa's after he calmed down. Anyhow, William ate dinner with the family and hung out for a while, then he came home to switch places with me so I could eat my Thanksgiving dinner and catch up with family. Everyone got turkey and sweet potatoes. There was no harm done. Like I said, we are now flexible people.

But our learned flexibility still won't lead us to grocery shopping like we used to do. After five years, I now avoid going to Wal-Mart with Ryder like the plague. It is bright, loud, crowded, full of too much for Ryder to look at, and full of rude people. This causes Ryder's senses to build pressure up like a rubber band being stretched too far. When his senses release that pressure, everyone had better watch out. Unfortunately, every human has to eat, so everyone has to get groceries, and Wal-Mart feeds our new-age need of immediate gratification since anything you need for your home, garden, or vehicle can be purchased at the same time you are buying food. But the effect of such a store as Wal-Mart is that it is a huge melting pot of all kinds of people in the same place, all seeking to satisfy their immediate personal needs. When you throw a child who gets overstimulated into the mixture, you will bump into "know-it-alls," "narcissistic loud mouths," and "opinionated poop-heads." Believe me, we have met plenty of them, and they are not just the shoppers.

A large store also echoes. Ryder is already pretty darn loud when he is upset, and some of his troubled moments in Wal-Mart have made me want to run over people with my shopping cart more than once. Total strangers have sneered at us, told us Ryder needed a spanking, or even come up to our shopping cart to tell him he is spoiled! REALLY!? (If anyone ever pulls out their cell phone to video Ryder having a fit that will be the last straw. I will be arrested and going to jail for assaulting someone with a bag of carrots.)

Seriously though, suddenly everyone is an expert in parenting, and in this world of social media, lots of people speak without thinking because they believe they can say whatever they want, when they want, to whomever they want.

I am all for freedom of speech, but whatever happened to minding your own business?

Chapter 18—If They Only Had a Brain...Or Some Manners

One afternoon, I was in the checkout line with Ryder and a huge amount of groceries for our family when he began to whine for some candy. The grocery store was bustling that day, and the lines were growing longer and longer, yet no other registers were being opened. The longer we stood in the checkout line the louder and more persistent Ryder's whining became. He had been in the bright lights, surrounded by strange smells, noises, and people for too long. He was tired and ready to get back to the familiarity of home. The huge amount of candy around the register was simply adding to his stress, playing tug-o-war with his mind.

There was a woman in front of me, unloading her shopping cart at the pace of a sloth, who started to chat with the cashier. They spoke openly about Ryder and me as if we were not there, as if I couldn't hear them. What idiots, chattering back and forth about how they wouldn't dare act like my kid when they were children because they knew better, their parents would've whooped their back ends, and on and on. I had an upset Ryder on one side of me, and I had these cackling hens on the other. I snapped. I knew my face was red because I felt all the blood rush to my head, and when my words spat out of my mouth, they were louder than I expected, even though I was restraining myself as best I could. "He has difficulty waiting for long periods of time because he is four and autistic!" is what I shouted at the women (shouted, even if from behind clenched teeth.)

There was silence from them (finally) and then the cashier said, "Well, there is nothing wrong with that." Then she said in a sappy, puppy dog voice, "Poor guy." UGH! (Can you see my extreme eye-roll right now?) Her response was enough to get my blood pressure back up again, but I held back from saying anything else. We just wanted them to shut up so we could get home.

When I told my sister-in-law about that day, she wanted to call the store to demand that cashier be reprimanded. Of course, I calmed my sis down and told her it was pointless, but her response made me think of how nice it would be if all large stores would take the time to train their employees about autism and how to act when they encounter a possibly autistic family experiencing a bad day.

If that's too much to ask, maybe they could simply require all employees to take a course in basic manners.

Part III

GETTING BACK UP

19

The Other Jennifer

OUR WORLD IS A BIT WILD, BUT I WAS SLAPPED IN THE FACE TODAY WITH a harsh reality check when I met another Jennifer and her four-year-old daughter, Sarah, at Ryder's make-up therapy session. This other Jennifer looked close to my age. Sarah is close to Ryder's age. Jennifer was already there when we arrived, and Ryder went to the back with his therapist. My eavesdropping ears perked up when I heard this mother make a phone call for the Medicaid Van Service because she had said her name was also Jennifer. Then I realized why a large car seat and a backpack were in the chair next to her. She didn't have her own transportation. (I have been without my own ride a few times in the past. If you have too, then you know it sucks. It sucks even more when you have children who need to be places, yet you are dependent upon others.)

The therapist brought Jennifer's daughter out to the waiting room when her session was finished. The two of them chit-chatted a bit, the therapist left the room, Jennifer began gathering her bags to leave, and then disaster struck. Something had triggered little four-year-old Sarah either right then or during the therapy session. Jennifer's daughter fell to the floor in a heap and began screaming the all too familiar yowl of an autistic child having a sensory meltdown. Tears were streaming down her face, and she ripped out her hair bow and sent it flying across the room as her agonizing cry continued. Poor Jennifer was struggling to pick her daughter and bags up at the same time so they could get outside to catch their ride. I stood up, snatched the hair bow off the floor, and told the other Jennifer I would carry the bulky car seat for her. Jennifer had tears in her eyes when she looked at me as I said this. I knew exactly how she felt, completely embarrassed, completely hopeless, completely helpless, completely *drained*.

We left the office and through the glass windows of the front of the building she could see her ride was not there yet. Little Sarah continued to howl and flail about in her mother's arms as her mother attempted to take a seat on a bench near the front door. Our therapy office is inside a large shopping center. It was Friday and busier than usual with shoppers coming and going. I set the car seat down for Jennifer and was going to head back into the therapy office, but I caught the all too familiar looks from people passing by. Jennifer and Sarah were receiving those harsh stares from strangers which implied, "What is wrong with your child?" or "That brat needs a spanking" or "Ugh, shut up!" There was no way I was leaving this little family alone to take that kind of beating. I told Jennifer (more like I hollered at her over the wailing) that I would sit there with her until her ride came and that way I could help with the car seat again.

So we sat there together. Little Sarah continued to claw and cry, occasionally giving a surprising kick to her mother's head or chest. She was a very strong little girl. Her mother was really struggling to hold her. I didn't want to be a nosey ninny, but wanted to help if I could, so I told her my son Ryder was autistic and that before he could speak he would have extreme meltdowns, too.

Jennifer told me Sarah was four and had just recently been diagnosed as autistic. I asked a few more questions and figured out really quickly that Sarah was completely non-verbal. Jennifer didn't know where to start to calm her daughter, fits like these happened on a regular basis, and Sarah had been in the public school special education class for going on two years. *Two years* of her four years of life Sarah was around "specialists," yet her own mother wasn't familiar with how to help calm Sarah, nor did she know what possible sensory issues her daughter had. (That system is so jacked up!)

I told Jennifer that Ryder liked to be held tightly while being rocked back and forth when he "fitted." Jennifer handed Sarah over for me to give it a try. Sarah's face was soaked with tears, she was sweating terribly, and she clung to

Chapter 19—The Other Jennifer

a dirty, faded pink baby blanket, which had large holes in it. Her small hands squeezed the blanket with all they could as the painful episode continued. I wrapped my arms tightly around her and began to rock back and forth, Sarah stopped screaming and flailing long enough to take a few deep broken breaths, but then she started back up again. Darn, I was hoping I had figured out how to soothe the poor child. I handed Sarah back to her mother.

We tried to communicate as best as we could while Sarah continued to fit. Most of the time all we could do was sit there and stare at the glass doors. What was taking her ride so long to get there? Time was *dragging*. Ryder's session that day was a forty-five-minute session, and I told Jennifer that if her ride wasn't there by the time Ryder's session was over, I would take them home.

Her ride arrived just as Ryder's session was ending. They brought Ryder out to me while I was carrying Sarah's car seat toward the large glass doors. Ryder had a perplexed look on his face as he watched Sarah who was still very upset. I put the car seat into the Medicaid van and told Jennifer to take care. Then Ryder and I walked hand in hand to my car. I could still hear Sarah while the van drove off behind us. Man. I felt numb.

During all of this, I was so amazed by Jennifer's patience, but looking back now, I don't think it was her patience that helped her sit there so composed while she was being kicked, hit, and screamed at by her child; I think Jennifer had plum given up. She may have caved in, but at least she wasn't kicking, hitting, or screaming back at her child.

There are cases of child abuse we hear about from time to time that involve autistic children. Evil things happen to theses innocent children, unimaginable things. Why do these terrible things happen? Do parents sit through fits like Sarah's day in and day out with no help, answer, or light in sight, and then just snap? Ryder's fits had been pretty bad for the first three years, but they had slowed down and become less frequent as time went on and he learned to communicate better, unlike four-year-old Sarah's. I can't imagine Jennifer's life. I look at Ryder today and thank God for our sweet, intelligent (yet very stubborn) autistic son.

Things in our life could be so much more difficult than they are.

Emerging From the Trenches

Please remember, when you see a family in a moment similar to the one I have described here, there is probably so much more going on under the surface. Please don't jump to conclusions or judge the people involved in the situation too harshly.

Some parents are hanging on to sanity by a small thread while they are literally being kicked in the head.

20

Double Ds and Triple Ps

P ARENTING GOES HAND IN HAND WITH POTTY-TRAINING, POOP, AND PEE: the Triple Ps. When Ryder was two and a half years old and Logan was a newborn, we also had to deal with the Double Ds, which is Double Diapers. Not only were the Double Ds costly, but the house smelled foul with a full pail of stinky diapers ripening daily. So the Triple Ps became a high priority on our list of things for Ryder to accomplish. It was a maddening (and expensive) *three* additional years after the birth of Logan before Ryder decided to end his diaper use. (Notice I said "he" decided.)

Our biggest hurdle with potty training was the fact that Ryder was terrified of the toilet, and he was comfortable with the routine of using a diaper. When we first put him on the seat, he acted like we were holding him down to saw his leg off. We needed to get him excited and interested in using the toilet. We bought a little blue stepping stool, then a Mickey Mouse padded toilet seat, and even a tiny real-life-looking toilet that made a cute flushing sound when we pushed the tiny silver handle. Ryder wasn't the least bit interested in using any of these items for which they were intended. I came into the bathroom one evening to check on him in the bathtub and Ryder had the padded Mickey Mouse toilet seat around his body acting as if the toilet seat was a swimming ring while he bathed. To my right, I saw that Ryder's giant Mickey Mouse doll was sitting on the tiny toy potty. (Apparently Mickey Mouse had to follow the rules and use the potty, but not Ryder.)

We tried to think of another approach. He loved Elmo so we bought the Elmo potty movie. Ryder watched it, but it didn't change his opinion about using the potty. We bought books which told a story of how much fun it was to use the potty like a big boy. Ryder sat down to look at the pictures while we read to him, but he still had no interest in being a big boy himself.

Ryder has always liked numbers and anything in order so I printed little pictures of how to use the potty, numbered the pictures, put them in order, laminated them, and taped them to the shower door next to the potty where Ryder couldn't miss them. Dawn sarcastically thanked me for the extremely descriptive instruction on how to wipe your behind that was slapped on an area in the bathroom where her friends could see. (Some of the more hilarious moments in parenting are the moments when you get to embarrass your children.) I told Dawn that I was glad to be of service. Ryder would go into the bathroom and count the numbers on the pictures. I believe he fully enjoyed them, but they didn't get his butt on the toilet. We even took him into the bathroom with us to sing a song and show him how it worked for us. He liked to laugh at us singing, but that was about it. We tried *everything* we could think of, to no avail.

Before we knew it, he was four years old, going on five, and still using diapers. Ryder knew when he had to use the restroom because he would say, "Purple monkey" when he wanted a diaper on so he could do his "business." There was a purple monkey on the front of the brand of diapers we used. But his knowing his digestive system needed relief still didn't get him on the stinking toilet.

One evening I was out shopping, and my husband was home with the kids. Ryder suddenly had to use the restroom and told his daddy, "Purple monkey.. Now I don't know if my husband couldn't find Ryder's diapers quick enough or if Ryder's digestive system was going haywire, but as I pulled up the driveway and stepped out of the car, I could hear Ryder yelling, "PURPLE MONKEY! PURPLE MONKEY!" over and over again with great urgency. He really had to go! William managed to get a diaper on Ryder by the time I made it to the front door where William was laughing pretty hard. The sight of Ryder running back and forth yelling "PURPLE MONKEY," is a memory to share with him with some day, maybe.

During the years we were attempting to get Ryder on the potty and out of diapers, Dawn watched a documentary on autism. In the documentary there was a twelve-year-old autistic girl who was still in diapers. Dawn pitied the young girl and pleaded with me to get Ryder potty-trained soon. But she knew as well as I did that we had tried almost everything except duct taping him to the toilet seat.

Probably a month after Dawn watched the documentary, I was leaning over the bathtub giving Little Logan a bath when Ryder walked into the bathroom, hopped up on the toilet seat, squatted like a monkey with his feet on the edges of the seat, and began to pee in the toilet! What??!! I was SO excited! Who cares if the way he was using the potty looked strange. He was using it! I realized then that Ryder had probably understood everything we had been showing him for the past three years, but his stubbornness must have been as unshakeable for him as for us.

His super-sized diapers disappeared from that day on, but Logan was still in tiny diapers so there was still some hint of Purple Monkey around. We hid Logan's diapers under our bathroom cabinet and did our best to keep them out of Ryder's sight. Ryder would still come to us and say "purple monkey" for a while, but we knew then he was capable of jumping onto the toilet seat, Tarzan-style, so we simply told Ryder that purple monkey was gone. "Purple Monkey gone." He would that repeat after us and threw a few short fits, but we held our ground. After some time passed, he stopped asking for the diapers. He did eyeball Logan's diapers whenever we were changing Logan, but that was it.

Did we overthink the solution and waste time, or did we not push Ryder enough? I don't know and again, I am at the point where I don't care. Spending time dwelling on that question is like asking, "How many licks does it take to get to the center of a Tootsie Pop?" The world will never know. Now Ryder has the Triple P's mastered, even though he still squats over the toilet like a monkey and he needs help with wiping. We will happily accept the compromise.

21

Ha-ku-na Ma-ta-ta

"You are a pushover." William told me while we were cooking together in the kitchen one evening.

"I am not a pushover," I replied, raising the knife I was using to chop garlic and pointing it at him in place of my finger.

"Yes, Jen, when it comes to disciplining the kids, you are a pushover," he nonchalantly repeated as he turned back to braising the meat.

"Whatever," I mumbled where he couldn't hear (but I knew I got the last word in.) I turned my attention back to chopping cloves.

This is the extent of argument between William and me. Massive amount of tension, right? After you've been with someone as long as we have been together, we are solid, we love each other, and arguments become more like discussions on *The Tonight Show*.

Our "argument" began because the kids did something crazy, and I chose to look the other way. I don't think I am a pushover. I think I am simply tired of getting upset over things that don't really matter. Most of the disciplinary procedures around here fall to me since William works away from home so often, and I can yell only so long until no one hears me anymore. Besides, I spent one too many years being stressed and angry while Ryder was a baby and young toddler. It is as if I woke up one day, looked into the mirror, and didn't like what I saw, so I decided to start a new diet and way of living.

Instead of kicking and screaming, I try to close my eyes and think before I speak slowly and clearly. I punish the older kids silently now. Their devices or remote controls will magically disappear and won't reappear until chores are finished or behavior improves. I ignore what bad behavior I can from the younger kids. They seem to calm down when they don't have an audience. Or they get a harsh and scary growl from me as they get put into time-out.

Every parent I know on a personal level believes in spanking their children. This is the South, after all, but none of them are raising an autistic child. I struggled with spankings for a while before deciding they were useless. Dawn became too grown to spank, and she never really did anything bad anyhow. Kay never felt the spankings even if I gave it all I had. Her little butt could be bright red and still she would laugh, yet she has always despised time-outs. When I spanked Ryder he just became very angry and the tension between us escalated to a point of ridiculous. I don't even know if he understood why I was spanking him, or if he just figured that I was abusive. Giving Ryder excessive amounts of praise when he does well helps him want to please others more often. If he is acting out for attention because he is angry, I ignore what I can or make him sit down somewhere secluded until he can calm down. Logan only learned to hit from the spankings he received. So I decided spankings were not worth the effort. Time-outs or privileges taken away are so much more effective.

The kids are home nearly every day with me, and they act like kids. Things will be spilt, broken, and used. The kids are also with *each other* nearly every day so there will be frustration, disappointment, and occasional rudeness or laziness. In the end, all of the material things that are ruined won't matter anyhow. What will matter are the memories the kids have and the lessons they have learned. I want a majority of their memories to be good ones and *all* of their lessons to stick with them for a lifetime.

Kay will never learn how to properly clean up a gallon of sweet tea from the kitchen floor if she doesn't spill it first because she was in too big of a hurry. Ryder will never learn how to properly chew gum if he doesn't get gum stuck in his hair and clothes. Logan will never take care of his toy guns if he doesn't break them only to find out that he will not get more until his birthday. Dawn

Chapter 21—Ha-ku-na Ma-ta-ta

will never learn to be responsible for completing her school assignments if she doesn't fail a few tests because she slacked off or procrastinated. I wasn't always so easy-going, but I now do my best to stay calm, cool, and collected even through the most outlandish times. My Mrs. Hyde has reared her ugly head in the past, and I have always regretted her presence.

When we moved next door to Mimi and Papa, we finally had a fireplace. William always wanted a fireplace. The fireplace room was one of the first rooms I unpacked and set up. I wanted it to be a manly room in the house where William could relax. I spent two entire days placing the furniture in the room, painting the wainscoting an earthy color, washing the pillows on the couch, scrubbing the couch clean, steam cleaning the carpet, wiping down the windows, putting up the asphalt grey curtains, and hanging all of William's impressive hunting trophies over the mantle. When the final day of man-cave decorating was over, it was late, and the room looked great. I left the girls to watch the boys while I took a much needed shower.

When I came out of the shower I heard Dawn say, "Oh my GOSH. Mom is going to be so *pissed*!" As I threw some pajamas on, my mind was going through all the scenarios which may have occurred while I wasn't supervising. Dawn was correct. When I came out of my bedroom and saw the fireplace room, I was pissed.

Ryder and Logan had gotten into the ash the previous owners had left in the fireplace. They were standing in front of the fireplace covered in ash from head to toe, no denying their guilt. An ash battle had occurred. There was ash covering the couch I had labored over, ash on the carpet I had steam cleaned, ash on the new curtains, ash stuck to the walls where the paint was still drying. Ash was everywhere! I started screaming. Both of the boys received a few whacks on the bottom and were firmly placed in the bathtub. I ordered the girls to stay in the bathroom with them and warned them *all* to not set foot out of it until I had the mess cleaned up.

I was cussing, scrubbing, and literally fuming while I viciously attacked the cleaning of the room with multiple vacuums and cleaning products. The kids heeded my warning and stayed in the bathroom the entire span of time it took me to re-clean the fireplace room. I believe they were honestly frightened.

But here is the thing. My friend called the next day to see how we were adjusting to the new house. She had raised five children of her own, and she was retired. All of her kids had grown and were living their own lives away from home. I told her what had happened the previous evening and how furious I still was. All she could do was laugh up a storm. She said, "That will be a great memory." I felt terrible since I knew the only thing the kids would take away from the night before was my outrageous reaction full of scary words.

The boys had never seen a fireplace before. I have never stopped them from playing in the dirt outside and they were being typical curious toddler boys. It wasn't as if the girls were not watching the boys. They were checking on them often enough, but the boys can destroy a room in 1.5 seconds flat when they work together.

The room was able to be cleaned. No one would ever know disaster had struck if I didn't tell them. The entire episode was not a big deal. It was not life threatening. If I could go back in time I wouldn't waste my energy getting so upset and then spend the night cleaning. I would smack each of the boy's hands and firmly tell them, "NO." Then I would tell Dawn and Kay to wash up their brothers while I went to find some wine. We would *all* get up at *dawn* to clean the room together, making sure no ash was left anywhere, especially in the fireplace. Hindsight is twenty-twenty.

There was one time I am proud I didn't over-react or jump to discipline. (You will get that pun in a minute) Jumping made Ryder happy from before he could even stand up. That boy would jump in his Jolly Jumper for an hour at a time, just smiling away. When he was old enough to have a twin bed in his room, he would jump on the bed so much that he jumped a huge hole into *two* mattresses. I didn't care, call me wasteful, but the jumping was keeping him happy and keeping us temporarily sane. Happiness and sanity are worth more to me than the price of a mattress. When we bought Ryder's third mattress, we also forked out the money for a huge trampoline for the backyard. Problem solved. We almost bought one of those trampoline beds, but I knew there would be no sleeping going on in the boy's room if we had done that.

I came to find out that Ryder's desire to jump is connected with his sensory input needs that should be met to give him a good foundation for the day. Part of his school day begins with either jumping on the trampoline or doing another proprioceptive activity that is similar to jumping. I would not have been doing Ryder any good if I had whooped him, scolded him for jumping, and taken away his mattress.

Chapter 21—Ha-ku-na Ma-ta-ta

It is not just my disciplinary style which has changed since we have been raising an autistic. The things I agree to do or refuse to do have changed. Placing an indoor trampoline and full-size swing inside my home makes total sense to me now, especially if it helps us get through bad weather days where Ryder will not go outside to play, yet needs to expel some energy.

I used to refuse to accept that I could not be in control of things in my house, such as what the kids ate for breakfast, how clean the house was, whether or not we would be on time to appointments, bedtime without brushing teeth, or leaving the house without make-up on. Now I refuse to care about all of the above because I have come to realize that I have *no* control over *any* of it. If we make it to an appointment within 10 minutes of the exact time with everyone in clothes other than their pajamas and fed (even if they had ice cream for breakfast), then I consider our goals met.

I am okay with hiding stockpiles of certain foods in my closet. It isn't hoarding now. It is called being prepared in case another hurricane floods Houston or an item Ryder eats is discontinued.

I refuse to demand Ryder sit at the dinner table with us. We make the invitation as special as possible, and he has enjoyed eating with the family a few times, but if he chooses to eat by himself, I don't care. He is eating.

The kids watch much more TV than I am comfortable with. One of the first things turned on in the morning other than the coffee pot is the TV. But I refuse to jump out of bed each day, flinging words of "don't do this or that" before I have had a cup or two of coffee. Morning life flows so much better around here if I am fully awake and caffeinated because then I am less likely to lose my temper as I transition the kids from TV zombies into schoolwork enthusiasts.

I would usually refuse to purchase expensive shoes for the boys because they grow out of them so quickly, but I couldn't refuse when Ryder persistently asked for the red Sketchers he saw in the shoe store window as we walked by. It was the first time he had shown an interest in anything he wore. The shoe store didn't have his size in red, but he didn't want silver or blue, he wanted the red shoes. I paid full price for a pair of shoes Ryder clumps around in everywhere he goes.

Ryder has naturally good manners and that makes him golden in the South where manners are still a big deal. For a child to say "no," to a typical mother around here would bring about a tornado of fur and a cry of "Release the Kraken!" The first time Ryder told me "no" when I told him to come back inside the house, I almost released my inner Kraken of fury upon him, but instantly realized it was the first time he had expressed his opinion in *words*. I was actually so proud, I refused to punish him other than correcting him with, "Say, no MA'AM."

When the sensory diet was explained to me, I had no problem taking fifty pounds of dry pinto beans and dumping them into a tub on our back porch. The beans are not for Ryder to eat, but for him to play with or even sit in. They provide tactile sensory input he needs to get through the day. Beans are all over the porch now and they are falling between the cracks of the wood. We will probably have bean plants growing up the side of the house by this summer. Oh well, how convenient it will be to simply pick beans from the back porch. I am sure it will keep the kids entertained.

I drove through McDonald's one evening, and the woman at the window asked us to pull forward to wait for the fries since they needed to cook a few minutes more. I will *refuse* to do that ever again. Ryder didn't understand why we were driving past the window without his receiving his fries. I had a friend riding shotgun with me that evening. It was the first time she had experienced Ryder's reaction to something he wasn't in agreement with. Whoa, was she speechless. Ryder calmed down, once the fries were delivered, but the next time I was asked to pull forward because the fries weren't ready yet, I refused. If holding up the line at McDonalds is going to help me keep my sanity and my eardrums intact, so be it.

The makers of *The Lion King* describe my current parenting style well in the song "Hakuna Matata." What a wonderful phrase. It's my problem-free philosophy. There is no perfect way to discipline or parent; therefore, it makes no sense to add extra stress and worry to my day while taking away years from my life.

Repeat after me, *Ha-ku-na Ma-ta-ta*.

22

Imaginative Play

IF YOU'VE EVER ANSWERED MILLIONS OF QUESTIONNAIRES FROM DOCTORS, studies, and therapy evaluations, while trying to decide if your child is on the spectrum, you would get the impression that autistic children are not expected to have an imagination or a silly side. At least, that's the impression we have had until recently. Ryder has proven this assumption to be very false.

They call it being unable to demonstrate "imaginative play." We had to check the box that stated Ryder lined toys up instead of making the toys move in a life-like way and check the box that stated Ryder liked to watch spinning tires on a toy truck instead of making the truck roll across the floor, and the box that admitted Ryder would totally freak out if something was put out of the order he had put it into. We checked a lot of other boxes, too. All of them made me feel like I was admitting our child was whacked beyond help because the questions made us focus on all the things our child could *not* do or chose to do *differently*.

Maybe an autistic child's brain wants to study, line up, and evaluate the toys *before* getting around to "demonstrating imaginative play." Or maybe the autistic child's brain sees a miniature car, calculates there is no probability of his riding in the car, and instead decides to watch the tires spin because spinning tires make more sense. Perhaps, we should see the need for order in the autistic's life as a sign they will grow to be a great help to the world because this world seems to be quite out of order. In the adult world, an orderly calculating brain would be considered highly intelligent and a major asset.

While I do understand these questionnaires help specialists determine at an early age whether or not a child may be autistic, I have often thought about how nice it would be if the questionnaire had a short "pick me up" at the end of them. Nothing too emotional because answering all of those questions about your child is emotional enough, but maybe a short line, such as "What makes each child different also makes each child special." Or "Even though your child might be different, it doesn't mean they are *less*." Perhaps, even an area where the parent can brag about the many awesome things their child *can* do.

I know it's a child's movie, but since I am on the subject of imagination, I feel it's appropriate to use Ariel from Disney's *The Little Mermaid* as a defensive example for the many uses a single item can have. Ariel was fascinated with mysterious human objects. She used the fork as a comb because the seagull told her that was what the fork was supposed to be used for. He was way off his rocker and Ariel looked ridiculous using a fork to brush her hair, but even after she had the chance to be around humans and study how they used the fork, she was still brushing her hair with the stinking fork. Maybe it worked for her. Maybe she also ate spaghetti and cleaned her fingernails with that fork. Either way, it worked for her.

One person has the right to use an object one way, while another person has the right to use the same object in another way when it's not harming anyone. Pinterest is fabulously popular because of this rule. Ryder's autistic brain likes to calculate, observe, and study an item or situation before making a move. That kind of brain seems odd to us for a child, but it should really be seen as, "Wow!" Ryder isn't missing out on being a child simply because he uses toys in a different manner than others. Toys are a free-for-all. Having toys to do whatever you want with them is one of the most appealing aspects to being a child, and kids shouldn't be told how to "properly" use them.

When we lived on the farm and Ryder went through his first evaluation, the therapists pointed out that he didn't want to play with the farm playset like other children, but they were all so amazed that Ryder was able to label all the farm animals in the playset and that he knew the sound each one made. Well, that's because he lived around the same animals at home. He saw how the animals walked, played, ate, and did everything else animals do. Three-year-old Ryder may not have wanted to play with the farm animals because he wasn't impressed with them. He saw them as ordinary. What he did want to play with was the giant tub of dry noodles they made available to him. Now *that* wasn't something he experienced every day, and he jumped right into the tub.

Ryder *does* have an awesome imagination, no denying that. I believe he has always had an imagination. His imagination simply emerged a little later than others.

- When William bought an electric globe for him on his fifth birthday (you know the thing you touch or speak into and the electricity follows your hand or sparks inside the globe) he went crazy for it. He couldn't get enough of it and he labeled it his "time machine" while he sat next to it giggling.
- He imagines he has a tail sometimes, waving a length of string or rope around him like he's seen animals use their tail to swat flies.
- He likes to put a blanket over his head to chase his brother or sisters around like a ghost saying, "Oooo. Spooky," laughing and running after them.
- Large empty boxes or empty laundry baskets become boats for Ryder.
- When he is outside, he will run around with his arms outstretched, flapping, pretending he is flying.
- He will create egg shapes with play dough and then use a box to make a nest for his eggs.
- He gets on the ground to pretend to be a lion roaring loudly, or hops around the room telling us he is a bunny rabbit.
- He likes to put socks on and pretend he is ice skating around the house.

Ryder has revealed all these forms of imaginative play as he has grown older and had a chance to evaluate the world around him. He can be purposefully silly, too, making farting noises, playing dead, or pretending to burp. He does not get these silly acts from me.

Unlike his delay in speech, I really do believe his gross humor is a traditional male thing.

23

Let's be Honest About Self-Esteem

IF WE ARE HONEST, MOST OF US SEE THE NEGATIVE OR IMPERFECT THINGS about ourselves when we look in the mirror. When I look in the mirror, I notice the birthmark on my cheek, the sagging of my skin, and the many extra pounds that snuck up on me after carrying four children, all of which taunt my confidence. Any evaluation of ourselves and by ourselves is usually critical just so. With impressionable daughters in the house I try not to make my imperfections seem like a big deal to me (even on the days they are). I always tell them it is important to love yourself, be able to laugh at yourself, and find the best in others.

A favorite social media post I read last April during Autism Awareness Month was a list of some of the positive attributes found in many autistic personalities. One of the top attributes was honesty.

Now Ryder is very honest about pretty much everything. He squeezes my extra tummy skin and says, "Squishy." (It drives me nuts, extra nuts when we have company over.) If we are in a public place and someone farts silently or smells a bit unclean, Ryder will be the one to loudly say, "Stinky!" while he sniffs around for where or from whom the smell is coming, totally oblivious to others' personal space. Even though he fears the consequences of doing something he isn't supposed to, he will not only admit he's done wrong, but will actually bring his wrongdoings to your attention. When he broke the screen in our living room window he brought me to the damage, showing me what he broke, even though his eyes were saying, "Please don't be too mad. I did such a bad thing. I know I did wrong." How could I be upset at a criminal who internally punished himself beyond any punishment I could've come up with by the time he confessed? Ryder's insistence to bring every hidden or embarrassing thing into light can melt my heart, make me want to hide under the table, or cause me to explode with laughter.

One of our daughter's more embarrassing moments, brought on by Ryder's honestly candid curiosity, happened at a dermatologist office. The office was so packed full of clients there wasn't even sitting room for everyone. Dawn was holding Logan and I was holding Ryder to help make some room for others. There was a sweet, elderly woman sitting right next to us. The boys were squirmy while we tried patiently to wait our turn, so Ryder and I were nearly on top of the sweet woman from time to time. But she just smiled as she watched my busy-bodied boys exude rudeness and myself exude contempt for whoever was responsible for over scheduling appointments that day.

Out of nowhere, Ryder reached over with his little pointer finger and poked a giant very hairy mole that was on the side of the sweet elderly woman's forehead. Exclaiming, "BEEP!" I was horrified. My daughter's mouths gaped open with shock, and they tried to become invisible from everyone in the room who had seen what happened. Little Logan actually shrieked with laughter. Thankfully, the sweet elderly woman laughed too, and so did her husband sitting beside her. She asked Ryder if he liked her mole because her grandkids did, and that's why she never had it removed. Although he didn't answer her, she kept smiling. In her many years, she had mastered what I try to teach my girls, to love yourself, be able to laugh at yourself, and to see the best in others.

So I was in the kitchen last night and Ryder came to me with a highlighter in his hand. He wanted me to follow him to the desk in the family room. (Keep in mind that part of his occupational therapy is to help him grip items such as pencils or buttons. He hasn't really done much writing on his own besides

Chapter 23—Let's be Honest About Self-Esteem

an occasional line or attempt at a circle.) I walked over to the desk with him, and when I looked down at the piece of paper lying there, I was surprised. Ryder had drawn a person! It was the most adorable stick person I have ever seen. It had an enormous head, it didn't really have a body, but it had stick legs, arms, hands, feet, eyes, ears, and a giant smile on its face. Ryder pointed to the stick person and said, "Ryder." He had brought me over to his self-portrait because he wanted me to add a hat to "Ryder." Once I was done with the hat I was instructed to draw "mommy and daddy" and once I finished them, Ryder exclaimed, "Family!" My heart burst. (That drawing is currently slap-dab in the middle of the refrigerator for all to see.)

Is that little stick person how Ryder sees himself? With a huge head and long legs? The wide grin on the stick person is my favorite part of the picture. It tells me that Ryder is honestly happy, and happiness is one of my greatest wishes for all of my children. I am ecstatic at his ability to show us he is self-aware through a drawing and I am curious to see what his future self-portraits will tell us.

One might say that happiness and self-confidence go hand-in-hand. With happiness being a great wish for all of my children, I try to instill confidence within them daily, and what better way to instill confidence than by accomplishment. How can one feel accomplished? By having a J-O-B.

Ryder's J-O-B at our house is to collect chicken eggs.

Chickens have been part of our life since Ryder was a baby. He loves our chickens. He will chase them around the yard laughing at their funky hobble-run. He has been helping us collect eggs since before he could walk.

There is nothing that compares to a farm fresh egg in the morning. Everything about a farm egg radiates nutrients and protein. The yoke is bolder in color and the shells are stronger. If you are ever in an egg race, use a farm egg, it takes a heck of a lot more to break the shell of a farm egg versus a store-bought egg. Our chickens free-range so our eggs are free from food chemicals which means they even taste better. At one point our chickens couldn't keep up with our egg consumption, and I had to purchase store-bought eggs. No one ate them. We had grown so accustomed to eating farm eggs, the store-bought eggs actually tasted like plastic to us. We bought a few more laying hens. Problem solved.

Now that Ryder is older, he is able to collect the farm fresh eggs on his own. He is very polite and if there is a hen in the coop when he goes to collect eggs, he patiently waits by the door until she is finished laying. Then he collects the eggs and runs them up to the house to place them into our egg bowl. He counts every egg as he adds them to the bowl. We have given him the title of Egg Collector, and he eats it up. Being the family's egg collector is his chore or job. It really gives him a sense of accomplishment and builds up his self-esteem. My goal is to stuff Ryder so full of self-esteem and self-worth that perhaps he won't be bothered by judgmental jerks he is bound to encounter in his lifetime. (I also hope to get him into martial arts so he can defend himself against the same jerks, if needed, but that's a chapter for another day.)

Going into the hen house to see if there are any eggs available gives Ryder the anticipation of receiving a present or surprise. It is a lot of fun to see his eyes light up when there are eggs to count. Because of his egg collecting J-O-B, Easter is by far his favorite holiday. Easter egg hunts were already such a fun game, but once Ryder learned Easter eggs are *special* eggs with candy and toys in them we had to mount multiple Easter egg hunts each year. I refill the eggs with exactly the same stuff Ryder collected in the previous egg hunt, and he doesn't care. It is the hunt he loves first; then it is the element of surprise when the contents are revealed. I could probably put dirt in an Easter egg and Ryder would still be ecstatically yelling, "Dirt!" once it is opened.

There are families of autistics who have started their own businesses to ensure their child has a job and a skill or trade later in life. I love supporting small businesses like those. We have a local coffee shop that is owned and managed by a family who has a child with a disability. They started their business to give their adult child a chance at self-employment. I will go out of my way to get a coffee from this shop to support what they are doing.

Maybe we should expand our hen house and add to our chicken population when Ryder is older and he can start a business selling farm fresh eggs to the community. It might not bring in a six-figure income, but I can think up worse ways for someone to earn a living.

24

My Precious

WE ARE BIG FANS OF J.R. TOLKIEN'S *THE HOBBIT* AND *LORD OF THE RINGS* books and movies. We couldn't find anything to watch on the television a few nights ago so we busted out the DVDs and decided to have a *Lord of The Rings/Hobbit* marathon. Whenever Gollum would appear on the screen we would holler for the kids who were not already in the room to come watch. Gollum is a unique and scary character in the J.R. Tolkien movies. His skinny, nearly naked hairless body, with humongous eyes, rotten teeth, and multiple personality disorder, add up to one creepy character and the kids all like to watch him, yet pretend they are frightened of him, too.

There is a part in the *Hobbit* where Gollum realizes he has lost the magical ring he calls his "precious." This ring has caused him a lifetime of extreme grief yet he continues to treasure it. The moment he realizes the ring is no longer in his loin cloth he freaks out. He shrieks and wails and flails and contorts his body in unimaginable ways due to the huge amount of anguish losing the ring has caused him.

I was watching this part of the movie when the similarity between Gollum's reaction and Ryder's reaction to losing something struck me. I strongly believe J.R. Tolkien derived his character Gollum from an autistic child. Gollum was acting *exactly* the same way Ryder acts when he loses one of his tiny treasures.

(Call me mean for comparing my son's behavior to such a character, but the truth is always more interesting than fiction, and I am not saying my son is *always* similar to Gollum, just sometimes. Sometimes I act similar to the Hulk, but deep down I am Cinderella. Don't we all have an alter-ego?)

His treasure that has driven us all the craziest is his "tiny red BB." "Red ball" is what Ryder calls it. It is a BB. It is literally the size of the top of an eraser on a pencil. Would it be easier for us to purchase a large container of red BBs? Yes, but that's how the BB problem originated. After Ryder had a BB rolling party in the house, I vacuumed up as many as I could find and didn't think twice about saving any. The BB he carries around now is the last lone BB he found behind the piano. We are clinging to the hope that some other small treasure will catch his eye and he will forget about the BB instead of breaking down and buying a large container of them because we would rather not have continuous BB rolling parties in the house. I guess we could hide the container of BBs, and every time Ryder thinks he lost "Red Ball" we could magically find it. That is a thought, but I am straying from the point I am trying to make here by comparing him to Gollum.

My point is that he dropped Red Ball in the backyard yesterday when I was raking up some leaves. Holy cow, it was the end of the world! Dawn came outside to see why Ryder was so upset and thankfully her young eyes spotted the tiny ball among the blades of grass and leaves. I would've never found it with my elderly vision. But up until the moment Dawn found Red Ball, Ryder had been in his underwear, hobbling around in a squatting position, crying and upset, while he frantically searched the grass for his precious red ball, acting *exactly* the same way Gollum in *The Hobbit* acts when he loses his "precious."

Autism is more common today than it was back in J.R. Tolkien's lifetime, but it was still around. I would bet money that J.R. Tolkien had been around an autistic child before or during the time he wrote his masterpieces. I have a hard time believing it is a coincidence that he so accurately captured the fit of an autistic child in the character Gollum without knowing what an autistic fit looks like. Our imaginations are simply exaggerated descriptions of the reality that surrounds us, right? That being said, maybe I should be writing a horror novel instead.

Not smiling? Oh, come on, where is your sense of humor?

Caution, Autism Ahead

Hear ye! Hear ye!
It's crazy over here!
It smells like poo,
And feels like goo,
You're brave to venture if you dare.

The babies all need changing,
There are smashed goldfish on the floor.
Chapstick smeared across the windows,
Oh, but wait, there is more.

Watch your step,
You just might slip
Thanks to Ryder's dish soap art.
Logan is digging in the trash
And tearing it apart.

You'll find more than wrappers in the couch,
So be careful where you sit.

Mom has left the water on,
I think her mind is in a pit.

The bathtub's overflowing,
And dinner's burning on the stove.
I think I hear a hurricane?
Nope, just the vacuum about to explode.

S.O.S might be too late,
But it's worth a try.
If we make it to tomorrow,
I will know God's a funny guy.

Jennifer Hayword
The early years

Before hands-free driving was a law in Texas, I was driving down a familiar road from our old house to our new one. We had just begun the moving process, and we were doing a ton of driving back and forth between houses as we cleaned out one house and cleaned up the other. The strip of highway I was driving on was secluded and beautiful. We passed a few ranches here and there along the highway, but most of the twenty mile route was thick woods of pine and oak. It was a pleasant fall day. I was on the phone with a family member who was in the hospital.

As I made a slight left going downhill, an enormous eight-point buck decided to jump from the woods and land on the blacktop right in front of my vehicle. There was no time to turn away or brake. We were cruising at a solid seventy miles-per-hour, and we hit him *hard*. I witnessed a moment of slow-motion where I saw everything that wasn't secured in my car (ketchup packets, goldfish, an empty water bottle, a pen) float up and then come back down as we came crashing on top of and then ran right over the giant suicidal wild animal.

Ryder was buckled in his car seat sitting in the middle of the second row of seats. He had seen the entire accident. Almost as soon as metal hit fur, we heard Ryder slowly say, "Oh. I'm sorry" with sincere empathy in his voice.

Chapter 25—Caution, Autism Ahead

An impact like the one we had just experienced is enough to shake up even the most confident driver, but with Ryder's response to the accident from the backseat all Kay and I could do, once the vehicle came to a stop, was crack up with contagious laughter. Logan had been sleeping and had continued to sleep through the entire ordeal.

I got out of my vehicle to assess our situation. The front end and left fender of my vehicle were totally wrecked, but the score was without a doubt Humans 1, Dumb Deer 0. A shiny black Dodge Charger pulled over on the other side of the road as I was staring in disbelief at the damage to my mom-mobile. I was trying to decide if it was still drivable. I had stuff to get done, and I really didn't want to wait for a tow truck, plus Ryder was already getting upset that the car had come to a stop and we weren't moving forward anymore.

A young man exited the Charger and ran over to us. He said he was a volunteer fire fighter and wanted to know if we were okay. Once I confirmed we were all fine, the young man began to quietly evaluate the damage to our vehicle. Then we walked behind my vehicle fifty feet back where Dumb Deer lay completely lifeless on the side of the road. It had been instant death for him. Not an antler was damaged on the buck's head.

"Your air-bags didn't deploy when you hit him?' Volunteer Firefighter asked in amazement.

"Nope."

"You have a large bar welded to the frame of your vehicle. The bar is what kept him from damaging the radiator. You are lucky he didn't come flying through the windshield. Do you want to keep the rack? We can call the game warden."

"No way." I chuckled disgusted at the thought. "You can take the rack and the meat. I don't want anything else to do with the creature."

Later on, safe at home, when I had a chance to sit and recap the eventful day, I realized something I had never thought about before. If we were ever in a major car accident, and I was either dead or passed out, Ryder would be at great risk. The girls would know what to do with Ryder, but what if they weren't with me? What if they were badly hurt and couldn't get to him? In an emergency situation, Logan would be shaken up, but he would be able to be comforted by a stranger, and he would understand enough to stay where he was placed until a family member could get to him. Ryder, on the other hand, would be a disaster of epic proportions. How would he react to strangers handling him? Loud sirens wailing? Strong smells of smoke or gasoline? Pain? The aftermath of the accident could be more disastrous than the accident itself.

After this series of "what-ifs" and nightmares ran through my mind, I googled until I found some window stickers for sale made for vehicles that carry autistic children. I bought two. The stickers are big, bright, and yellow and inform whoever needs to know that there is an autistic child on board who might react strongly or wander off in an emergency situation. There is a whole series of similar window stickers, seatbelt covers, and accessories made by creative geniuses available for purchase online. (Smart, smart people. Thank God for the creators of such items.) I also made sure my cell phone had my ICE numbers slapped across the screen lock picture in large clear font.

The kicker is that the giant stickers are shaped like a caution sign, and I think the word "caution" is actually on the sticker. When we came out of the store one afternoon and we were searching for my car, Kay said, "There is your car. I can see the "Beware of autistic child" sticker on the back."

LOL! I was rolling! Beware of autistic child? I guess I can see how it looked like a warning for other people from Kay's point of view. After all, she would know firsthand just how scary and wild living with an autistic child can be. Of course, I corrected her and explained the reason behind the massive window sticker, but I really admire her innocence, and I deeply appreciate the humor that her point of view brought me.

Finding the humor in everything stressful—now there is something which makes sense when you are raising an autistic child.

Somewhere during the transition of getting accustomed to being an autistic family, I realized we wouldn't make it out alive without this sense of humor. There are so many opportunities to laugh about the craziness, and laughter *is* the best medicine!

Here is a small dose:

When you have company over and in the middle of a conversation your autistic child's shriek of excitement from the bedroom causes your guest to jump from the couch, poised to run for it because they believe the noise was

Chapter 25—Caution, Autism Ahead

the smoke alarm, you don't flinch at the all-too-common noise. It's worth a good laugh.

When your autistic child, who is learning to speak, has been watching back-to-back episodes of *Peppa Pig* now speaks with a British accent even though he is 100 percent Southeast Texan, you have to laugh.

When you are potty training your autistic child, and you come across brown stuff on the wall in the hallway, your natural reaction is to lean over and sniff the brown stuff, only to find it is dried chocolate ice cream art, not poo, you are appalled, relieved, and *then* you laugh.

When you have been outside working in the garden for hours and you come in the house ready for a nice hot bath, but there are tiny plastic toy animals placed side by side all around the outside rim of the bathtub, you carefully step over them into the tub of hot water. While you soak surrounded by zoo animals, you laugh.

When someone tells you how your autistic child will eventually eat the healthy food in front of him if you don't give in because the child won't starve himself, you really break out laughing to the point of passing out.

When your autistic child is saying, "Moose! Moose! Moose!" yet you and everyone over for the barbeque hears, "Boobs! Boobs! Boobs!" you all have to laugh, even your son.

When you come across a stranger in the store who will not leave you alone until your autistic child gives them a high-five, but instead your child spits a mouth full of water at them, you are horrified and quickly push the shopping cart out of the store (but you laugh later.)

When your car is so nasty from the daily mess of fries on the floor board, the diaper changing station in the back, and the constant spills from sippy cups that in your rushing you accidently leave your door wide open in a downtown Houston parking lot *all day long*, then come back to find the car is still there and nothing is missing, you throw a fist in the air with thankfulness. Then you laugh at the filth which deters robbers.

When you have to make a phone call to your autistic child's dentist to tell her that your son has somehow ripped off the metal spacer she glued to his capped tooth and you believe he swallowed it, you wait for her to process the information. Then you both laugh when she tells you she has never had a child do such a thing, and she doesn't see the point in putting another spacer in.

When you are leaving the local Christmas parade, but your autistic child is not ready to leave, and as you drag his limp body hanging from the stroller toward your car with him steadily screaming, police officers directing traffic follow you with their eyes as if you are a kidnapper. You smile sickly and quickly get your kid to the car to hide his screaming. Then you laugh at the possibility of getting arrested because you know a stint in jail with three meals and a private cot might feel like a vacation. You are strongly tempted to yell out the window as you drive by the officer, "I kidnapped him!" You laugh.

Somedays I daydream that our life is being manipulated by a television network and that people toting cameras and microphones will hop out of the bushes any moment to tell me Ryder's autism is a hoax and this life we have been living is all part of a complex reality show. I find myself laughing out loud at the thought of how much insanity other people *would* have seen if our life really was reality TV. I can't tell you how many times William has turned to me and asked, "What are you laughing about?" Hah! If he only knew what goes on inside my head!

26

Amazingly Autistic

I KNOW I COMPLAIN A LOT ABOUT AUTISM. HONESTLY THOUGH, ADJUSTING to autism hasn't been the easiest part of our lives. More than once I have reached the point where I say I *hate* autism. I despise parts of autism, but I adore my son completely. I am amazed by my son as often as I am perplexed by him. And that's pretty often.

My oldest son's first word was not a simple "dada" or "mama." He was a little over one when he said his first word—"dinosaur." Of course, that's *all* he said over and over again for a long time, but no one can deny his passion for those extinct creatures. He loves dinosaurs and never gets tired of playing with dinosaur toys, looking at dinosaur books, or watching dinosaur shows. I picked up a toy dinosaur from under the couch once. As soon as Ryder saw it he said, "Dyoplosaurus." I looked it up later on and he was correct! Once he learns the name of a dinosaur, animal, or insect he is interested in, he won't forget it. That brain of his is amazing!

By the time he was two-years-old, he had memorized entire dances from the *Just Dance* video game, and he would dance the entire jig when a certain song came on. Some of my favorite memories of young Ryder are of him punching the air and bouncing around like a boxer while he danced to his favorite song, *Eye of the Tiger*. His memory is out of this world. He will watch an entire movie once, quietly take it all in, and then have it memorized forever. As a one-year-old, he wasn't speaking the dialogue in his favorite movies, but he was making the *sound effects* of dishes dropping, squeaking, hiccups, or musical pieces on the movie, right before they happened. We have a lot of DVDs. Ryder has his DVDs memorized down to what they look like without their cases.

Similarly, he doesn't forget a place or a route. If we turn left at a certain red light in town he might holler from the backseat where he wants to go simply because we turned left, but he knows turning right would bring him to his desired place, even if it is two hours away. That's pretty awesome and entertaining.

At two, Ryder began putting items in order by size or lining items up in color patterns. He had me rolling Playdoh into balls over and over again one evening. I was on the couch watching TV and he would bring the Playdoh to me, wait for me to roll it into a ball, then run off with it. Then we heard Kay yell, "Mom! Dad! You have to come see this!" Ryder had about ten of the Playdoh balls lined up not only in order by biggest to smallest on the bedroom floor, but he had only used the blue and purple Playdoh balls for his line up so the balls in order from biggest to smallest were also in a pattern of blue-purple-blue-purple. For a boy who just turned two and was barely speaking, that was pretty impressive.

By the time Ryder was four-years-old he knew all of his ABCs and the sounds that each one of them makes. Since then, he has been putting together small words on his own. For example, he spelled B-U-G with his blocks the other day and was shouting, "Bug! Bug! Bug!" in the living room while pointing at his word. We all came running, thinking there was a dreaded Texas-sized red wasp in the house. Once he had us all watching him, he then spelled F-O-X with his blocks. I was amazed beyond words and just started texting everyone I knew. At this rate I am thinking how nice it would be if he taught himself to read. That is something I wouldn't put past him.

Then there is his relationship to water. He has always enjoyed being in water. Water is pretty much all he drinks as well. If he receives a new toy he particularly likes, he *insists* on introducing it to water (battery powered toys don't last very long around here). After his love of water lead him to the pond at a young age, we were very concerned about the danger that pools, pond, lakes, and creeks presented. But because of his love for water and the high water bill we were paying with all the baths he was taking, we embraced his

Chapter 26—Amazingly Autistic

love of water, and he flourished in it. He taught himself how to swim before he turned five. He taught *himself*. All we did was provide the pool and some supervision. That is award worthy as far as I'm concerned.

Ryder is a true music lover. He loves average songs such as nursery rhymes, one-hit wonders such as *What Does the Fox Say*, all kinds of classical music, and a few days ago he wandered into the kitchen humming a Lady Gaga song. But it is Johnny Cash that really gets him clapping to the beat. Ryder has a deeper voice than most kids, too, similar to Johnny Cash's. We listen to Johnny Cash's greatest hits on the way to therapy to get Ryder in a good mood. *Folsom Prison Blues* is the song we always have to start with and *Daddy Sang Bass* is the song we listen to as we pull into the therapy parking lot. I have no singing voice, and when it is just Ryder and me in the car, I also have no shame. I sing along to Johnny Cash as loudly as I can. The best ride to therapy was the day Ryder chimed in from the backseat, "In the sky, Lord, in the sky!" at the end of *Daddy Sang Bass*. Ryder's singing voice is the best.

He has an extremely impressive eye for detail. Ryder has a massive collection of tiny animals he has collected since birth. He likes to line his animals up in pairs and then march them onto a toy pirate ship. Out of his massive collection, he will correct me if I dare to put the wrong animal onto the pirate ship. The giraffe I picked up when I sat down to play with him looked to be the same size, shape, and color as the other giraffe, but Ryder *knew* which one was its correct match. He must count the spots on the giraffe or the wrinkles on the elephant because they both looked the same to me, but by now I have accepted I am simpler minded than he in some areas.

Ryder's physical strength is right up there with Captain America. At age three he wrapped his little arms and legs around a wooden pole the diameter of a coconut tree and shimmied straight up with no effort. He can hug you so tightly your breath is taken away and you literally start to turn purple. When he was outside a few summers ago and got upset, he picked up our metal chairs and started chunking them across the porch. That was a bit distressing, but since he was only *three*, it also made me consider training him for weight lifting contests.

He had us going one day because he was humming Bach or some other composer's work while his pointer finger hopped along the lines of the paper with the musical notes on it. "Is he reading this music?" I shouted at Dawn with excitement to get her to come look at what Ryder was doing. "No, that's not the song he is humming," she told me. Was I a little let down because my son wasn't reading classical sheet music at three? Nah, I was proud enough of him for pretending to read it while he hummed the melody. That makes him creative.

I love that both Ryder and I share a love of sleep. I love sheets and comforters, pillows and nightlights, a cold room and a fan blowing in the background, and so does Ryder. A parent I was chatting with at therapy told me her daughter didn't sleep. I know sleeping is a common problem with children on the spectrum, so I am forever thankful to God for making Ryder a sleeper. That is a hobby we will share for a lifetime.

When Ryder first started receiving speech therapy, his therapist told me not to worry about teaching him, "thank you," "please," "you're welcome," or any other polite words. I was a bit shocked. She explained his main goal was to learn to say, "I want ____." Basic language skills were our focus point. Well, Ryder simply picked up amazing manners on his own. He actually *enjoys* being polite (unlike other children I know who are his age). That makes our son a natural born Southern gentleman.

He is autistic. He is also amazing. Consider the fact that our son has been in battle with the world around him since birth, yet he still manages to wake up with enthusiasm each new day. You can see why we admire Ryder.

Would he be just as amazing if he wasn't autistic?

Of course, he would be. He's our son.

27

PB&J Posse

My daughter asked me the strangest question the other day. First she gave me a few examples of some sweet families we know (who I am a bit suspicious of because they seem to have perfected parenting). She pointed out that each one of them have a "theme" to their family. We know a family heavily involved in horse breeding and rodeos—they are the Horse Family. Another family is very musical. Every one either sings or plays an instrument—they are the Harmonious Family. Another family we know is super healthy and they work out together daily—they are the CrossFit Family. After bringing these families and their nauseating perfection to my attention, Dawn asked me what *our* family theme is.

Family theme?? Hah!

Half of us are unusually introverted, the other half abnormally extroverted. We are all screamers, tear jerkers, pouters, and door slammers. Some of us are sassy and some sarcastic. None of us can ever agree on where we should go for vacations or what we should do on the weekends. We are all good at something, but each thing we are good at as individuals, no other person in the family excels at. We are all opinionated and stubborn, arguing our different views until we're blue in the face. We vary in what type of pets we prefer, foods we eat, music we listen to, colors for Christmas decorations, politics, and religion.

We don't have a family theme. What we have here is a *posse*. Our family posse reminds me of a good ole' peanut butter and jelly sandwich. We are chock full of nuts, a little sweet and sticky, yet salty with soggy white bread, all slapped together in one gooey mess of unexplainably perfect coexistence.

Once PB&J are merged, they are fully committed to each other.

One thing is for certain. We are a family that is *seriously* committed. I don't just mean committed as in "insane asylum" committed. Yes, we're all a bit crazy, but we stand by each other through any circumstance like soldiers on a battlefield. How do I know this? Because we have stood together through the challenges autism has brought us. Autism has made our bond stronger. It has made us see each other at our most raw and most vulnerable yet we still love and tolerate each other. I am confident there will be no man, woman, or child left behind here, especially when it comes to the PB&J bond our children have.

Our kids fight each other the way all siblings do, bashing each other physically, emotionally, and mentally to the point of me either issuing death threats or chasing them out of the house with the broom. But they won't put up with anyone *else* bashing a sibling. They have their own exclusive secret organization within our family posse. It has one solid rule: Only those who hold the title of Brother or Sister have the privilege to do harm to the others. The spark which sprouted the roots to this special bond was having an autistic brother.

Having an autistic brother has made my children much more compassionate for others, too. If someone tried to tell me one of my children was bullying another child, especially a disabled child, I would *never* believe it. Even if they had video, I would insist the video was tampered with. When you live with and love an autistic person, you can't help but see how our differences make us all of more worth than society would have us believe, how every human not only has a desire to be loved, but *deserves* to be loved, and how each of us have feelings which can be hurt.

I have a theory involving the expectation of autism rates skyrocketing over the next decade. I theorize that with the rise of autism diagnoses, we will see a decline in bullying, and, hopefully, in school shootings. The more children in this world who have autistic siblings, the more children there will be who have learned compassion for others, as my children have. Wouldn't that be wonderful?

Chapter 27—PB&J Posse

We had some friends over a few years ago, before Logan was born. All the kids went outside to play tag or hide-and-seek, as usual. At one point, one of the kids told Kay that her brother was "crazy." Kay was friends with the child who made that statement about Ryder, but she got in the girl's face (which was a sight since the other girl was at least a foot taller). With her hands on her hips, her face in a scowl, and a stern voice, she warned the older girl, "Don't *ever* talk about my brother like that again."

Kay had been punched in the face by a boy about a month before for some disagreement, and I had told her then that she shouldn't dish out what she couldn't take in return. I was pretty impressed that she had the cojones to stand up for her little brother to a much taller and older girl, knowing full well that if the older girl had decided to challenge her, she might be in for another punch in the face.

The girls know how to describe autism if someone asks, "What is wrong with your brother?" This has happened more than once because at first glance Ryder looks like any other child. They tell them nothing is wrong with their brother, that he is autistic, and all being autistic means is that his brain is wired differently than most other people's brains. Then they usually go on to give an example of how powerful Ryder's memory is or how funny he can be. Their answer pretty much leaves the other child with nothing left to say or ask.

Once Logan was born, he was automatically initiated into the PB&J Posse, and he draws the line to defend his older brother. Ryder was being scolded last week by Kay and two-year-old Logan charged Kay with a long stick, hollering, "You leave my Ryder alone!" I was in the kitchen laughing inside. I had to immediately text William about the battle line that had just been drawn within the ranks.

The girls know I am concerned about what will become of Ryder if he is not an independent adult by the time I am no longer around. Of course, Dawn, being the oldest, always reassures me that Ryder will not be forgotten or neglected once my husband and I are gone. Both of the girls have also stated that if any suitor wants their hand in marriage, he had better be more than willing to accept Ryder, or the deal would be off. This concern is a ticking clock in the back of my mind, reminding me that I cannot stop or control time. I will not be here forever to keep my special-needs child safe. Tick, Tick, Tick, Tick,

Tick ... The pressure of time I feel isn't an exaggeration of my smother-mother personality.

It's a rat race for autistics out in the world. When I heard about a state-funded program Ryder would qualify for if he needed help as a young man finding a job or learning how to live independently, his pediatrician told us to sign up *immediately* because she heard there were waiting lists for the program. Thank goodness I made that call because she was correct. The waiting list was a *twelve-to-fifteen-year* waiting list by the time I signed Ryder up last year.

Twelve to fifteen years will fly by quicker than I would like. Already I look at Logan and I can't believe he is two-and-a-half. He is an absolute Godzilla on most days. His hobbies are smashing it, throwing it, climbing it, hitting it, kicking it, or screaming at it. "It" is any person or thing in his way or in his hands. If Logan has anything large or long in his hands, all the kids scatter in multiple directions for fear of being bludgeoned.

Watching Logan romp around causes me to think to myself how we were absolutely bonkers to decide to have another baby when Ryder was Logan's age. When Ryder was the age of Logan, we were dealing with his constant meltdowns and really wild autistic stuff was coming out of the woodwork. Most people would have sworn off having any other children while going through what we were. Perhaps we were beyond exhaustion and beyond thinking realistically at that point in our life, so we threw caution to the wind, said, "Why the heck not?" and made another baby.

Having a fourth child was one of the best irrational decisions we've ever made. I study how our PB&J Posse interact with each other daily, and I feel a bit relieved. I know we will all not just look out for Ryder but also for each other for the rest of our lives. Every time I hear that anxiety-causing Tick-Tock Clock in the back of my mind, I know in my heart that our kiddos will take care of each other once Will and I are no longer around.

Then my heart is able to tell my mind to "Shut up."

28

The Four Letter "F" Word

F.E.A.R *(Forget Everything And Run)*
or
F.E.A.R. *(Face Everything And Rise)*

I SAW THESE COMPARABLE ACRONYMS ONLINE SOMEWHERE. I THINK THEY are fantastic. We all experience fear. How we react to our fears shapes us individually; therefore, fear is actually important. It is not simply a second-hand emotion.

Ryder has a fearlessness of water which completely contradicts his fear of more everyday items or common occurrences.

When Ryder was one, he began to shriek from fear while he was in his room. I ran into the room to see what the matter was. He had climbed six inches off the ground onto the top of his miniature piano. He must have felt as if he was six stories off the ground because he was scared to the point that he couldn't budge.

Ryder loves elephants, but he was completely terrified of an alphabet-singing elephant toy we purchased for him the Christmas when he was two. Ryder would see this toy and from his reaction you could believe it was possessed by a demonic spirit. We had to keep it in the closet until we gave it away. He knew it was in the closet, too, so he wouldn't step foot in there until it was gone.

Then there are the scary elevators. Ryder calls the elevators "rocket ships," and he squeezes his eyes shut while clinging to me like a baby monkey on its mother's back whenever we have to ride an elevator. That results in a lot of strange looks and laughter from fellow elevator riders.

Most of us would shrug off or laugh at the things Ryder fears. But his fears are not less real than any of ours because fear is personal. Fear knows no boundaries, nor does it discriminate.

There are things I fear which Ryder laughs at, like the nasty caterpillars which plague our area annually. Ryder will fearlessly grab a handful of the fat caterpillars from the ground and bring them into the house to laugh while I scatter to the far corners of the house trying to escape the semi-monstrous snake-like beasts he holds.

New foods, changes in routine, introductions to new people, places, sounds, smells, or sights—these are all battles Ryder constantly faces. He knows he has to face these fears each and every day, yet everyday he wakes up with a smile. Sure something might trigger a meltdown the moment he sets foot out of the bedroom, but he doesn't let that stop his curiosity or hope of what a new day may bring.

Ryder is going on six as I finish up this little book of madness. We have all come so far over the past years, but he has definitely come the furthest.

When Ryder heard we were going to the store last month he was excited to go with us because our dog had destroyed his favorite toy elephant, and he told me, "Store, elephant, store?" William and I exchanged side glances of uncertainty, but how could we resist? Ryder was asking so nicely. We took a deep breath and prepared for the worst.

When we arrived at the store, Ryder refused to sit in the shopping cart. "Here we go," I thought. "We will be the spotlight of the store as I am chasing him around the entire time or when he decides to ball up into a corner I can't remove him from." But Ryder walked beside the cart while we picked out what we needed to get. He waved at every person we passed and told them each "Hello" with a smile. He picked out his replacement elephant when it

Chapter 28—The Four Letter "F" Word

was time and sneaked two other toy animals into the cart, too, but we didn't care. We were speechless through the entirety of the shopping trip because of how well-adjusted he was.

Ryder agreed to let us cut his hair a few days ago in exchange for a cheese pizza from Domino's. William was honestly messing with Ryder when he struck up the deal to possibly shave his shaggy mane. Neither of us really expected Ryder to agree to a haircut, and as he voluntarily sat down on the bathroom countertop with a towel wrapped around his little shoulders William looked over to me and asked, "Is this really happening?" Ryder was still shaking with fear as the clippers ran across his head, but he remained on the counter until we were finished. The end result was the best-looking haircut Ryder has ever had. After his bath to remove the excess hair, Ryder rubbed his hand across his newly shaved head a couple of times, and said, "Ryder the hedgehog." What a trooper!

Ryder has also strayed from his fast-food fry addiction. He now is more than happy to accept frozen fries baked in the oven served in a red basket. I apologize for those with stock in McDonalds reading this who now realize why their profit margins have decreased.

He handled transition *very* well last week when I had to interrupt his therapy session to grab him and run out the door to get William to the emergency room. William had almost sliced his fingers off when a power tool jammed up on him. I told Ryder we had to go because Daddy had a bad boo-boo. Ryder was initially upset but didn't put up too much of a fight when I explained that he would get to swim in Mimi's pool soon. That sudden interruption and change in schedule would have caused a volcanic eruption from Ryder just a year ago.

Ryder makes me one very proud momma with how well he is handling his fears. Becoming a mother shaped me and filled my soul with a joy and contentment that I wasn't even aware existed. Being a mother of an autistic son has strengthened and refined me not only as a mother but as a human being. Raising autism has brought me to the battlefront against my own fears.

For the past five years I have been fighting fears which have crept up on me—fear of myself, fear that autism will not let Ryder have the life he desires. Fear whispers to me, "Do you have enough endurance and patience to continue with what it takes to help Ryder? Will Ryder ever hold a job, find romance, or his niche in life?"

Emerging From the Trenches

I have clashed swords against common fears somehow amplified in me, such as fear of failure or fear of change. Fear speaks in my mind: "Are we doing enough? What happens if the world's demands and expectations for Ryder become more than he can deliver? Won't it be easier to continue life in isolation, not pushing the limits set before him?"

Then there are the fears which stage surprise attacks: The fear of peoples' ignorance or violence toward something they don't understand. Fear stirs hard emotions deep within me asking, "Will Ryder ever encounter authorities who violently jump to conclusions? Will he be able to protect himself from abuse delivered by people who are supposed to be there to help him?" Did you see the news footage of what those "friends" of that autistic man did to him? They tortured him!

Fear can be the worst kind of disorienting enemy. If it is left unchecked, it can greatly degrade my quality of life, which in turn impacts my family's quality of life. The only solution I had at the beginning of this battle was to dig metaphorical battle trenches to better defend my sanity and my family. The trenches provided me with a feeling of safety and a place to strategically gather my thoughts.

But a trench is not meant to be a permanent place to dwell, and this battle with autism is far from over.

As I enter this new chapter in my life, I feel as if I am emerging from my battle trenches with a renewed sense of purpose and energy. Ryder is hoisting himself up and over those trenches daily with such courage that I can't help but follow after him. His bravery enables me. I can feel the battle-worn soldier I used to be fading in memory and a new battle-*ready* soldier taking her place.

I will emerge from these trenches with my family by my side. I will use my second wind to recover what was lost and rebuild what was damaged. I will fight now as a seasoned warrior with a mightier set of weaponry.

My weapons will be humor and laughter, knowledge and disclosure, imagination and acceptance, my words and my unconditional love, what experience has taught me and sometimes…just choosing to look the other way.

Considering *who* and *what* I battle for, I cannot afford to allow fear to overpower me, so I fight on.

Because surrender is not an option.

Afterword

Dear Ryder of the Future,

This book was written to open the eyes and hearts of strangers, not to degrade you. Nor was it written for us to receive pity.

Every moment over the past six years has been worth it. Every moment over the past six years has been very special to me. I look forward to every moment to come that we share together. You are loved beyond words.

As you navigate this world, Mom wants you to remember a few things:

First of all, your version of autism is yours, and it is nothing to be ashamed of. Just like an Olympic athlete is gifted with special capabilities, you are gifted, too. Make the most of the gifts you have been given.

Second of all, every single person on this earth has setbacks, not just you. Don't let your setbacks keep you down or make you an angry person. Some of these setbacks will be delivered by people who do not understand your autism. So stand tall. Find the humor in every moment that takes you by surprise. Find something worthy in every person. Educate people who are open to learning while ignoring people who choose to remain closed-minded.

Lastly, LIVE IT UP! Broaden your horizons and embrace the strange. Try new things and spit them out if they don't suit you. Go different places and come back home when you need to. Fall down and get back up, no matter what. Push yourself to really experience everything this world has to offer, the good with the bad.

Oh, I almost forgot. Remember to brush your teeth well. Wear deodorant when you are of age. And try to wear at least a pair of underwear when answering the door.

I love you.

Love,

Mom.

Acknowledgements

Many thanks to all who made this book a reality, P. Ross, C. Carr and the entire Hugo House Publishers, Ltd crew. Your support in this endeavor was phenomenal and unforgettable.

Thanks to all my family members who helped shape and review this work from beginning to end.

My greatest thanks goes to my sister, Nora. Thank you for being the shining star you naturally are. Your light not only pulled me past the boundaries of a mundane world I was slipping into, but helped me remember who I am and brought back my love of self-expression through writing. Sisters forever, no matter how far.

About the Author

JENNIFER HAYWORD LIVES IN WOODSY SOUTHEAST Texas with her husband, four children, and dog Sookie. She courageously homeschools all her children, including her autistic son, Ryder. Jennifer believes in the strength of family, the innocence of childhood, the importance of free speech, the avocation for human rights, and the freedom to protect all of the above.

Contact the Author

Because she would love to hear from you!

Have something personal to share or a question to ask?

Email me: haywordjennifer@gmail.com

Curious to see what our everyday life looks like?

Follow me on Instagram: @emerging.from.the.trenches (Jennifer Hayword)

Feel like exploring Pinterest with me?

Find me on Pinterest: @haywordjennifer

Want more of what you just read?

Connect with my blog through www.emergingfromthetrenches.com

www.ingramcontent.com/pod-product-compliance
Lightning Source LLC
LaVergne TN
LVHW041337080426
835512LV00006B/493